FOLLOW THE LEADER

FOLLOW THE LEADER

Dan Schmidt

VICTOR BOOKS™
A DIVISION OF SCRIPTURE PRESS PUBLICATIONS INC.
USA CANADA ENGLAND

FOLLOW THE LEADER is a study of the Book of Matthew for high school students. It focuses on Jesus and His disciples and is applied to discipleship for followers today. Student activity booklets (Rip-Off Sheets) and a leader's guide with visual aids (SonPower Multiuse Transparency Masters) are available from your local Christian bookstore or from the publisher.

Scripture taken from the *Holy Bible, New International Version,* © 1973, 1978, 1984, International Bible Society. Used by permission of Zondervan Bible Publishers. Other Scripture quotations are from *New American Standard Bible* (NASB), © the Lockman Foundation 1960, 1962, 1963, 1968, 1971, 1972, 1973, 1975, 1977.

Library of Congress Catalog Card Number: 86-60880

ISBN: 0-89693-629-5

Recommended Dewey Decimal Classification: 248.83
Suggested Subject Heading: YOUTH—RELIGIOUS LIFE

© 1986, SP Publications, Inc.
All rights reserved
Printed in the United States of America

Contents

One / THE GAME FOR LIFE
7

Two / A LEARNING EXPERIENCE
18

Three / BUILDING A BETTER YOU
28

Four / PRAYER: LEARNING FROM AN EXPERT
41

Five / HITTING THE ROAD
52

Six / IT'S A MIRACLE!
63

Seven / FLYING LESSONS
72

Eight / THE POINT OF PARABLES
83

Nine / A CLOSER LOOK
93

Ten / I LOVE A PARADE!
104

Eleven / CHOOSING THE CROSS
116

Twelve / AN EMPTY TOMB
131

*To Sue, who encourages me
to jump in with both feet.*

THE GAME FOR LIFE
Matthew 1:1–3:12

CHAPTER ONE

When I was a kid, one of my favorite games was follow the leader. We'd play in parks, pools, and playgrounds; but the rules were always the same: to imitate precisely what the guy at the front of the pack was doing. Eventually I grew tired of those antics. I could only hop on one foot, turn somersaults underwater, and go down a slide backward for so long. I got older and went my own way.

A few years later, when I was in high school, I took the game up again. But the players were different, and unlike my experiences as a kid, the leader no longer changed every few minutes. I began following a very different Leader: Jesus Christ.

I've joined a line of players that reaches back nearly 2,000 years. History shows me that the game is worthwhile. I find myself looking back more and more to see how some of those early players did, to learn about their triumphs and failures.

For the next few weeks, we're going to study this game together. We'll look at some of the participants, review the rules, and most important, get to know the Leader. As we do this, my hope is that we'll move from study to action. After all, everyone knows that playing is better than spectating.

The Official Handbook

Each of the four Gospels describes the life of Jesus. One of these, the Gospel written by John, takes an approach which is quite different from the others. Of the three remaining "Synoptic" (from two Greek words for "same view") Gospels, only the one written by Matthew comes from a member of Jesus' original 12 followers.

We know a little bit about Matthew from details we can piece together out of the various Gospels. Before Jesus came along, Matthew worked for Rome. He spent each day sitting at a table flanked by burly Roman soldiers, collecting money from travelers. This was a common sight in Israel—just one of the many countries occupied by Roman forces. Normal Roman procedure called for heavy taxation of all subjects, and generally, the Romans used national citizens to collect taxes.

Tax collectors were feared and hated. They were often dishonest men who were out to make a profit for themselves. Because they had protection, they could and would charge more than Rome actually required. After all, who would argue with a couple of armed guards? As a result of this, tax collectors were regularly shunned by their own people.

When Jesus invited Matthew to follow Him, Matthew experienced a dramatic change in lifestyle. He left the big house, the parties, and the good life of a Roman employee to become a disciple. He decided to follow Jesus. Just like that.

What drove him to make that decision?

A Leader Worth Following

Matthew stresses the importance of his Leader right from the beginning of his book. He does this by providing a copy of Jesus' genealogy. Since this may seem at first glance to be an incredibly boring way to begin, we need to ask why Matthew would lead into the best story he knows with something that might turn off his readers.

The answer (and you may not believe it) is that some people find history interesting!

A few years ago, the miniseries "Roots" was shown on TV. One installment of that series now ranks as the seventh most-watched TV program of all time. "Roots" started a movement which swept the country. All of a sudden, people wanted to find out about their ancestors. My own brother wrote letters to Europe and spent hours in remote city halls tracking down family records.

This interest in roots is not new. The people of Matthew's day were fascinated by their ancestors, particularly ancestors who played a part in the development of Israel.

Matthew's opening comments are easier to understand when we see them in light of a prevailing interest in family trees. When Matthew links Jesus to Abraham and David (1:1), he refers to figures known throughout Israel. Abraham was the father of the

Jewish nation, and David was its most famous king. Jesus' impressive lineage would be like someone today having George Washington and Ulysses S. Grant for great-great-grandparents. And that's not all! As Matthew is quick to point out, the rest of Jesus' genealogy reads like a *Who's Who in Israel*.

The opening chapter of Matthew shows the impressive credentials Jesus enjoyed. But ties to patriarchs and kings did not make Jesus a person for whom Matthew would drastically alter the course of his life. As Matthew goes on to tell us, there are other reasons to follow the Leader.

Shattered Silence

The last book of the Old Testament was written about 430 B.C. After that, God was silent for four centuries. That silence was broken with the appearance of an angel who announced a particular birth. Matthew picks up the story here.

This angel did not visit a prominent city, like Jerusalem, Samaria, or Rome. He did not speak to a king or religious leader. Instead, this messenger from God came to a small Galilean village and spoke with a blue-collar worker, Joseph of Nazareth.

Matthew focuses on Joseph more than the other Gospel writers do because he is so interested in discipleship and obedience. Both of these concerns come out in the account of Joseph's encounter with the angel.

Joseph was newly engaged. Then he found out that his fiancée was pregnant. After giving the matter careful thought, he decided to end the relationship without making a fuss. But then an angel stepped in to disrupt his sleep. He told Joseph to do two things, both guaranteed to cause problems for the carpenter.

First the angel said: "Do not be afraid to take Mary home as your wife because what is conceived in her is from the Holy Spirit" (1:20). In a small town, news of Joseph's decision about Mary would have traveled fast. Besides the inevitable gossip, he might easily have faced a slacking off of business when customers learned that his fiancée was pregnant.

Second, the angel informed Joseph: "She will give birth to a son, and you are to give Him the name Jesus, because He will save His people from their sins" (1:21). The name "Jesus" was common in Joseph's day. It was the Greek equivalent of the Hebrew name "Joshua," the name of one of Israel's famous generals. Not only did the name recall a well-known historical person; it also meant "savior."

Can you imagine the flak Joseph took when others heard his choice of a name for the new baby? It was bad enough that the child was born under questionable circumstances; but then Joseph had the audacity to name Him after one of Israel's great leaders. What's more, with that name the father was suggesting that the boy would be some kind of savior. The idea!

Joseph was in a dilemma. On one hand, an angel (an *angel!*) came with a message from God, telling him to stay with Mary. On the other hand, Joseph was pressured by those around him to take a different course of action. It would have been easy and socially acceptable to abandon Mary completely.

So how did Joseph choose to handle the difficult situation?

He obeyed God.

From Joseph's obedient response, we learn a great deal about his character. Even though we do not see him again in Matthew's Gospel, we have the impression from these few verses that here is a man worth knowing and imitating. Matthew calls Joseph a "righteous man" (1:19), a description linking him to others like Noah and David who also relied on God for help in tough situations. When God spoke to Joseph through the angelic messenger, this righteous man listened and obeyed.

Choose or Refuse

Joseph was not the only recipient of a special message from God. Matthew tells us that some dignitaries from the East also received an unusual call. "We saw His star in the East and have come to worship Him," they said (2:2). These men went first to Jerusalem for further directions. Instead of receiving a warm reception, however, the visitors caused a stir among King Herod and his counselors. These politicians were up to no good, as Matthew quickly shows.

Herod's first tactic was an attempt to enlist the magi as spies. He asked them to bring back a report of what they found in Bethlehem. When days turned into weeks, Herod finally realized that the men weren't coming back. (They too saw an angel!) So in a rage, the king ordered the deaths of Bethlehem's baby boys.

This seems unthinkable to us, but it was in line with Herod's generally nasty character. Josephus, a Jewish historian in the first century, says that Herod passed on this violent nature to his son Archelaus, who later ruled Judea. No wonder Joseph decided to live somewhere else when he brought his family back from Egypt (2:22).

By introducing Herod and his cronies, Matthew deftly brings out the choices that are available to any person; one can either follow the Leader, or attack Him. The magi from the East chose to follow Jesus, as we see from their intent to worship Him. Herod and the religious people with him chose another path. Matthew draws the lines clearly.

Obviously, Matthew wants his readers to follow the example of Joseph and the magi. An attitude of obedience and worship is far better than one of malice and disdain. At the same time, Matthew is realistic enough to know that some, like Herod, will do all they can to fight against God.

Before we move on to more of the story, let me pause to point out another aspect of Matthew's style. Have you noticed how often he quotes from the Old Testament? He refers to Old Testament portions frequently (1:23; 2:6, 15, 18). We need to get a feel for why the Old Testament is so important in this Gospel.

Something Old, Something New

Imagine you're in the process of writing a term paper on Louis XIV. What would your approach be? If you wanted to pass the class, you wouldn't sit in front of the TV with a notepad in your hand and jot down the first thing that popped into your head. Instead, you'd go to the library and look for some good books on

French history. Then you'd read them, looking for information that would help with the paper. If you came across a particularly good quote, you'd include that in the paper and footnote your source. That way, your work would take on an air of authority, as you referred to recognized experts in the field.

When Matthew wrote his biography of Jesus, he too did some research, using a tool that was at his fingertips: the Old Testament. With it, Matthew gained acceptance from Jewish readers. He was also able to show how Jesus fulfilled Old Testament prophecies about God's promised Saviour. Matthew's purpose was to show that Jesus was the Messiah; fulfilled prophecies were submitted as evidence.

A prophecy from the Book of Micah fit into Matthew's story to tell where the Saviour would be born.

> *But you, Bethlehem Ephrathah, though you are small among the clans of Judah, out of you will come for Me one who will be ruler over Israel.*
>
> Micah 5:2

And Jesus was born in Bethlehem.

According to Matthew, Jesus' early years also fulfilled other Old Testament prophecies. One of these comes from Hosea 11:1, as quoted in Matthew 2:14-15. These verses follow the movements of Joseph and his young family:

> *So he got up, took the child and His mother during the night and left for Egypt, where he stayed until the death of Herod. And so was fulfilled what the Lord had*

said through the prophet: "Out of Egypt I called My Son."

Hosea originally referred to the whole nation of Israel with this verse, but Matthew later takes the verse to mean something slightly different. For him, the Lord was speaking not about a large group, but about a single Person—Jesus, the Messiah.

Matthew bases his interpretation on a principle that you may have already encountered in a civics class. If you're up on your politics, you know that a senator serves as a representative of people from a particular area. Matthew has this same sort of thing in mind when he talks about Jesus acting as the representative of His people.

Matthew relates how Herod ordered the killing of all the boys in Bethlehem and the surrounding area ages two and under. And he includes another reference to the Old Testament:

Then what was said through the prophet Jeremiah was fulfilled: "A voice is heard in Ramah, weeping and great mourning, Rachel weeping for her children and refusing to be comforted, because they are no more."
Matthew 2:17-18

He draws this prophecy out of Jeremiah 31:15. Like the verse predicting Jesus' birthplace (Micah 5:2), Matthew and his readers understood Jeremiah 31 as "messianic." That is, it was a portion of the Old Testament which clearly spoke about the Messiah whom God would send. We'll see other messianic verses in Matthew, and I'll point them out, so tuck this one away in your memory banks.

Jeremiah 31 is basically upbeat. It describes the Lord's intention to restore His scattered people, and there is just a hint that His action will involve some pain and heartache.

Matthew picks up on the hint. Looking back on the early years of Jesus' life, Matthew sees the hardship He faced right from the beginning. Matthew realizes that even with the coming of God's Son, bad things still happen to innocent people. What Matthew affirms is that good will come eventually. He quotes from a passage that promises restoration of God's people after a time of disaster.

Another Leader?

Remember, Matthew has decided to follow the Leader, and he wants us to know why. He begins by telling us that the Leader is an important Person from a human standpoint. That's not all—this Leader is also important from God's perspective. He is announced in a dramatic way—through an angel and a star—and right from the beginning others want to follow Him. Joseph willingly obeys God's directions as given by an angel. The magi eagerly search for the King of the Jews in order to worship Him.

Matthew looks next at John the Baptist. If anyone should have been a leader, it was John. He came up out of the desert almost like a mirage, dressed in camel's hair and a leather belt, a connoisseur of bugs and honey (3:4). Not only did he look and act unusual; he also delivered a fiery message reminiscent of Old Testament prophets: "Repent, for the kingdom of heaven is near" (3:2).

People flocked to hear him. All this attention might have gone to John's head. How would you respond if suddenly entire cities of people were hanging on your words? But John knew exactly what he had come to do: he was a messenger, preparing the way for the Lord, one about whom Isaiah prophesied (Isaiah 40:3). John called attention to Someone else, not himself: "After me will come One who is more powerful than I, whose sandals I am not fit to carry" (Matthew 3:11). This desert man, it turned out, was not the awaited Messiah. He was not the Leader, but a follower—like Joseph and the magi.

Do you sense what Matthew has done? He has written about the Leader whom different people have chosen to follow. Matthew described some reactions, both positive and negative, to this Leader, all the time siding with Joseph, the magi, and John.

Who is this Leader worth following? He is the One Joseph was not ashamed to provide a home for, the One the magi worshiped, the One toward whom John the Baptist pointed: Jesus of Nazareth.

A LEARNING EXPERIENCE
Matthew 3:13–4:25

CHAPTER TWO

Matthew, a former tax collector, gave up a lucrative job for a game of follow the leader. But this was no ordinary child's amusement—the game placed high demands on those who played it. Matthew wrote a book in which he described several other followers, people like Joseph, the magi, and John the Baptist. All of these—Matthew included—gave up money, security, or popularity in order to follow a new Leader, a Person they considered worth committing themselves to.

The Leader Himself comes into view in the third chapter of Matthew's Gospel. There we see Him coming to John on the banks of the Jordan River.

The Baptism of Jesus

Try to picture this scene in your mind's eye. The Jordan was nothing like the Mississippi or the Amazon; in many places it was only a few yards wide. Desert crowded right up to the river with just a few patches of foliage separating rock and dust from the

18

water. There, somewhere just north of the Dead Sea, throngs of people came to be baptized by John. Jesus was one of those people.

John recognized Him immediately, and tried to deter Jesus: "I need to be baptized by You, and do You come to me?" (3:14)

This is remarkable! John knew that he was not the Leader, but one sent as a forerunner of Jesus. When He finally did arrive, John tried to shrink into the background. His only response was one of great humility: "I need to be baptized by You."

Jesus realized that a certain plan must be carried out, so He gently challenged John to do his part. When John did finally baptize Jesus, the die was cast. There was now no turning back for either man.

As soon as Jesus was baptized, He went up out of the water. At that moment heaven was opened, and He saw the Spirit of God descending like a dove and lighting on Him. And a voice from heaven said, "This is My Son, whom I love; with Him I am well pleased."
Matthew 3:16-17

How do you suppose the people watching all this reacted? Most likely, more than one dropped over in a faint. Then to make matters even more dramatic, Jesus suddenly left the scene and went to the desert (4:1).

At the very moment of triumph and affirmation by God before the watching crowd, Jesus was taken to face one of the most difficult experiences in His life.

Remember now that Matthew is describing our Leader. He wants us to realize that Jesus is indeed

God's Son, which he shows by recording the events that surrounded Jesus' baptism. And now Matthew intends to show that Jesus is mightier than Satan.

According to Hebrews 4:15, Jesus' experience with Satan prepared Him for leading you and me to God. That verse says: "We do not have a high priest who is unable to sympathize with our weaknesses, but we have One who has been tempted in every way, just as we are—yet was without sin." The high priest here is Jesus, and the temptations He faced include those described for us in Matthew 4:1-10.

Since Jesus faced the kind of trouble that you and I encounter, our study of this portion of the Book of Matthew should reveal some principles which will help us today.

Face-off

Satan's first remark delivered a severe blow. Jesus had been out by Himself in the desert for over a month, away from grocery stores and restaurants. He had fasted for 40 days and 40 nights. With classic understatement, Matthew says that "He was hungry" (4:2).

Standing near Jesus, Satan pointed to the round smooth stones that littered the landscape: "If You are the Son of God, tell these stones to become bread" (4:3). The taunt was two-edged. First, Satan tried to make Jesus doubt the clear assertion that God made earlier ("This is My Son"). Second, Satan appealed to Jesus' hunger with a reasonable-sounding statement. What would it hurt? Who would know? Why not use some miraculous power for self-satisfaction?

Jesus found an answer for the tempter in Scripture.

21 / A LEARNING EXPERIENCE

> *Jesus answered, "It is written: 'Man does not live on bread alone, but on every word that comes from the mouth of God.'"*
>
> Matthew 4:4

(This quote is from Deuteronomy 8:3.) Jesus showed Satan that He was driven by a power greater than His stomach. Another follower of Jesus, the Apostle John, remembered that Jesus said similar words on another occasion: "My food is to do the will of Him who sent Me" (John 4:34).

Satan tried a second time to thwart Jesus. Taking Him to the highest point of the temple, Satan urged Jesus to jump. Imagine the crowds that would gather to see the sight! And the opportunities to preach when Jesus would come floating down on an angelic parachute! Again Jesus went to the Bible (Deuteronomy 6:16) for help. He said: "Do not put the Lord your God to the test" (Matthew 4:7).

For Him to give in to Satan at that point would have been to test God. It would be like standing on a railroad track in front of a speeding train and counting on God for protection. The lesson of Scripture is that God does indeed care for His own, but He protects them from unexpected harm, not that which is self-inflicted.

Finally, the devil paraded all the world's kingdoms before Jesus. Because he is the prince of this world, they were his to give. But God's plan was for Jesus to conquer and reign, not to be given these things as part of a deal. Satan tempted Jesus to speed up God's timetable.

The price for this "gift" was too high. Satan said,

"All this I will give You, if You will bow down and worship me" (4:9). Jesus commanded Satan to leave, with an authoritative word ringing in his ears: "Worship the Lord your God, and serve Him only" (4:10; see also Deuteronomy 6:13).

After Jesus' obedience to God—even to the point of dying on the cross—the Apostle Paul could write:

Therefore God exalted Him to the highest place and gave Him the name that is above every name, that at the name of Jesus every knee should bow, in heaven and on earth and under the earth, and every tongue confess that Jesus Christ is Lord, to the glory of God the Father.

Philippians 2:10-11

Jesus was content to fulfill His purpose and live according to God's schedule.

What does this episode teach those of us who want to follow Jesus? First, we learn that Satan is not an unconquerable foe. Second, we should see that for God, the end does not justify the means. In other words, even though we may have some legitimate goal in mind, we are not free to reach that goal in whatever way we want.

All the things Satan asked Jesus to do were, in a sense, reasonable. The problem was that Satan wanted them done his way and not God's way.

Like Jesus, we too can go to the Bible for help when we are tempted to think or do something that is wrong. Jesus lived out the principle of James 4:7: "Resist the devil, and he will flee from you."

So far we've seen Jesus' impressive lineage, met

some people who chose to follow Him and others who refused, and witnessed His triumph over Satan. With all this laid out for us, we are ready to trace the rest of Jesus' earthly ministry. The first 3½ chapters of this Gospel cover about three decades of Jesus' life; the remaining 22½ chapters describe less than four years.

Looking for a Few Good Men

Jesus was on His own. John the Baptist was in prison (Matthew 4:12), and the crowds had gone home. The work was then to begin. Jesus started to preach, using a message John began: "Repent, for the kingdom of heaven is near" (4:17).

A few listened and began to follow along as Jesus spoke. From this group Jesus selected a small band. He chose to pour Himself into 12 men rather than to spread Himself thinly over a multitude. Naturally, He picked the best and brightest of Jerusalem's elite.

Or did He?

Jesus didn't go to the local university to seek out top graduate students. He didn't head downtown to find the sharpest business minds. Neither did He enlist the most popular or the best-looking folks available. Instead, He went for a walk on the beach and called two pairs of brothers.

All four men were working at the jobs they did every day. Jesus' call to them was like other calls God gave to people in their ordinary routines. Think of Moses, tending sheep when he saw a burning bush (Exodus 3). Gideon was threshing wheat when an angel invited him to save Israel (Judges 6). Then there was Elisha, who was preparing his fields for planting when Elijah came looking for an assistant (1 Kings 19).

Interruption of the daily routine, such as happened for all these people, should tell us that God won't necessarily wait for a special time to talk with us. Each moment of the day—whether you're eating breakfast, riding the bus, sitting in class, or mowing the lawn—is important. Even when you're on Christmas vacation, God can speak. The challenge for us is to be ready to hear.

No one time is sacred for God. Sometimes we think that He should wait until we're at camp or in church before He asks us to do something.

Moses, Gideon, and Elisha were immediately affected by their encounters with God or His messengers. The same is true for Jesus' first disciples. It was as though they had been waiting for something to happen. As soon as Jesus called, "they left their nets and followed Him" (4:20).

Are you waiting for God to call? You may not see an angel in the cafeteria or find Jesus sitting at a desk in study hall, but do you keep yourself open? Are you listening expectantly?

The original disciples displayed an eagerness to hear God. When Jesus came, they were willing to listen and obey. They didn't ponder a long time and put off a decision; they went and followed the Leader.

When Jesus spoke, the disciples listened. They followed Him on a journey that took them all over Israel and through all sorts of experiences. They learned firsthand what sort of person their Leader was by spending every possible moment with Him.

I grew up in the Bahamas, and spent a lot of time on the beach. The ocean was a part of life. Some of my friends could accurately predict the weather just by looking at the sky and sea. This wasn't the result of guesswork, but of many hours spent outside, watching and learning.

It's the same for those who want to learn what God is saying and how He is speaking. Time is important, necessary, critical—time for praying, reading and studying the Word, and time in church with others who know God well.

Teacher, Preacher, Healer

Matthew's next lines give an overview of Jesus' ministry:

> *Jesus went throughout Galilee, teaching in their synagogues, preaching the good news of the kingdom and healing every disease and sickness among the people. News about Him spread.*
>
> Matthew 4:23-24

Three things in particular stand out in these verses. The first is that *Jesus was a teacher*.

First-century Israel had no public schools with labs and full-court gyms. If a young man wanted an education, he attached himself to a teacher like an apprentice does today to a craftsman.

Teachers, or rabbis, were experts in the Jewish Law, and they attracted large followings of pupils eager to glean pearls of wisdom. Often these students would sit at the feet of their teacher, soaking up his comments on Moses or the Prophets.

Jesus adopted this pattern with a few modifications. First, instead of waiting for people to come to Him, Jesus selected His own followers: "You did not choose Me, but I chose you," He told them (John 15:16). Second, Jesus was not above addressing large crowds in an informal setting. Finally, Jesus did not stay aloof from His disciples. He ate, slept, talked, and cried with them for three years. They shared each other's lives and developed a relationship far deeper than what was possible for a traditional rabbi and his pupils.

The second thing we see in this passage is that *Jesus was a preacher*. Have you noticed a difference between preaching and teaching? Teaching imparts knowledge from one who knows to one who wants to learn. Preaching shares life experiences. It can be full of fiery exhortation, or it can be earthy, done with genuine and evident concern for the listener. Jesus used both of these approaches in His preaching.

I think of Jesus as a teacher when He is with His 12 disciples, telling them about Himself and God. Jesus the preacher is evident when He addresses the crowd (Matthew 15:10) or criticizes the religious leaders for their hypocrisy (Matthew 23).

Third, we see that *Jesus was a healer*. More than any other activity, Jesus' healing ministry demonstrated His interest in people. Matthew often shows Jesus among a group of sick men and women. Jesus healed because of His compassion, and often His healing included touching the one who was ill.

By reaching out to a leper or a blind man, Jesus did something that very few others were willing to try:

He ministered to those who were neglected by society. Jesus walked into the middle of sickness and disease and offered hope with His touch. The miracles of His healings produced joy and often led to widespread conversion.

Does Matthew's portrayal of Jesus sound appealing? Imagine having your favorite teacher (surely you have *one!*), the best pastor you've known, and the person who is most interested in your needs—all rolled into one. Can you begin to understand how Matthew felt about his Leader?

As we go on to the next chapter, we're going to see Jesus in His role as teacher. A little later on we'll examine His ministry of healing. And along the way we'll notice His preaching methods. So hang on as we move into the heart of Matthew's Gospel, Jesus' Sermon on the Mount.

BUILDING A BETTER YOU
Matthew 5:1-12

CHAPTER THREE

George and I were best friends in high school. We did everything together: took pictures for the yearbook, water-skied from dawn until dusk, and collected shells. We also enjoyed riding and tinkering with old bikes.

One summer, George decided to build his own 10-speed, starting with a frame someone had thrown away. It took weeks of cleaning, adjusting, and fitting new parts before the bike was ready to ride. Finally, George had a prize: a glistening black 10-speed that rode smoothly and fast.

Christians have a lot in common with that black bike. At one point we were more like rusty frames, not good for much at all. But then Jesus reclaimed us. And now He is in the process of restoring us, making us into something useful again.

Jesus' Sermon on the Mount tells us about that restoration process. Turn to Matthew 5 and look at the opening 12 verses.

It's important to realize that this sermon was given to Jesus' disciples (5:1). This doesn't mean just 12

29 / BUILDING A BETTER YOU

men; in fact, there were many more than 12 disciples. Let me illustrate this with a picture:

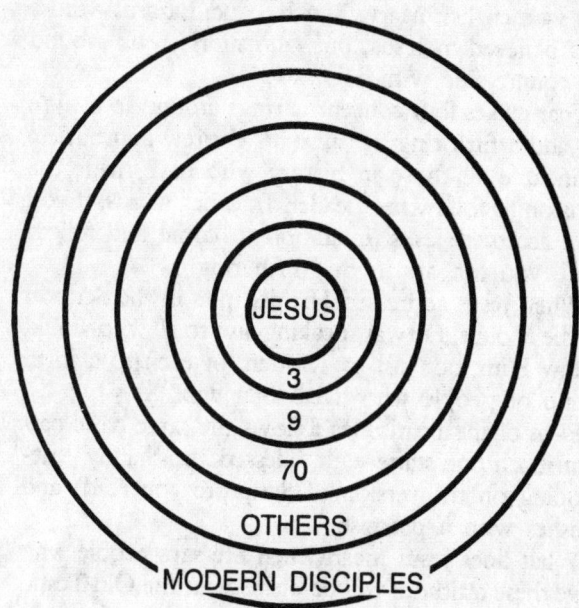

In the center circle stands Jesus, who calls people to follow Him. All who answer the call become His disciples. Three men were especially close to Jesus: Peter, James, and John. Nine more were also members of His special band (these nine plus the three comprise "the Twelve" disciples). But wait! There's more!

Luke recorded a time when Jesus sent 70 people

out on a mission (some manuscripts say 72). These people were certainly disciples (Luke 10). And finally, there was a group of disciples which included men and women like Mary, Martha, and Lazarus—those who believed in Jesus, but who didn't walk around the countryside with Him.

That makes four concentric rings around Jesus. We can add a fifth ring, because it's entirely appropriate to include all those in history who have made the decision to follow the Leader. In other words, if you have accepted Jesus' invitation to come and follow Him, you too are in that fifth ring.

When Jesus addressed His disciples in the Sermon on the Mount, He was speaking also to all who would follow Him, not just to 12 men, or even to a small group of people who lived long ago.

Each of the Beatitudes follows the same basic pattern. Each one starts with "blessed" or "happy" (depending on the version of Scripture you read) and finishes with a promise.

What does Jesus mean when He says people who have these attitudes will be blessed? In the Old Testament, blessing indicated pleasure and often brought with it some reward. When God blessed people, He showed His interest in them and promised benefits for them. One of the most famous Old Testament blessings appears in Numbers 6:24-26:

The Lord bless you and keep you;
the Lord make His face shine upon you
and be gracious to you;
the Lord turn His face toward you
and give you peace.

God's shining face indicates His pleasure, and the blessing also includes a promise of peace.

Jesus' Beatitudes follow in this line of blessing. Speaking to His disciples, Jesus encouraged them to lead lives that honored God. He promised His followers rewards when they finally would meet God.

Eight Beatitudes (from the Latin word for "blessed") lay out Jesus' expectations for His followers. Let's look at them now.

Down to the Metal

Blessed are the poor in spirit, for theirs is the kingdom of heaven.

Matthew 5:3

The first thing my friend George had to do in building a new bike was to scrape off the rust. Unless he went down to the bare metal, paint would never stick to the frame and other parts attached to the frame would also rust.

Disciples are like that bike frame: they must first get rid of something before they can add what will make them useful and complete. The first Beatitude addresses this.

"Blessed are the poor in spirit." Jesus doesn't say, "Blessed are those who give away all their money and become poor." His statement deals with the spirit, not the bank account.

I recently read about a man who spends his time restoring old barns in New England. Not only does he do this for people who hire him, but he also buys run-down barns for himself, just to fix them. An interviewer writing the story quoted this man as saying, "I'm barn rich, cash poor." This man had a lot of barns; what he didn't have was a lot of money.

Reading about that man reminded me that no one can be rich in everything. There is always a trade-off. Because Jesus wants His followers to be rich in one thing, they must be poor in another. A disciple, says Jesus, must be poor in spirit.

Dependence on Jesus

This means that followers of Jesus can no longer rely on their own strength or ingenuity to get by in life. Peter—for all his cleverness as a fisherman—still couldn't hope for anything of lasting value until he gave himself over to Jesus. In doing this, he became poor in spirit. He put down his own desires and tendencies and let Jesus take over. By becoming poor in spirit, Peter, like every disciple, could discover true riches.

These riches are to be found in the kingdom of heaven. So says Jesus in the second half of this Beatitude. When a disciple gives himself up to Jesus, when a follower hands over the reins of his life to the Lord, then God is able to work in that life.

How do we become poor in spirit? By redirecting our lives. We need to take our eyes off ourselves—to stop thinking about how competent, strong, rich and good-looking we are—and look at Jesus. Only as we begin to understand His desires for our lives will we be "God rich and self poor."

A Layer of Tears

Blessed are those who mourn, for they will be comforted.
Matthew 5:4

The first step in this new direction is difficult: we must mourn. Does Jesus want us to cry? Well, yes, in a way; but crocodile tears won't do.

The sort of mourning Jesus is talking about comes through the disciple's awareness of sin. Jesus wants His followers to realize that sin, no matter where it is found, grieves God. This should in turn make us sad. If there is sin in my life (and there is), God is sad. If there is sin around me (and there is), God is also sad.

Should I mourn forever? No. Rather, I must *recognize* the sin in my life, be moved when I realize how it grieves God, and then seek a remedy. This was the Apostle Paul's solution when he looked at himself and found some things he didn't like: "What I do is not the good I want to do; no, the evil I do not want to do—this I keep on doing" (Romans 7:19).

Examination of his life pointed up weaknesses for Paul and made him mournful. The sin in his life drove him to depression. He went so far as to cry out: "What a wretched man I am! Who will rescue me from this body of death?" (Romans 7:24)

But Paul did not wallow in depression. He knew the solution to his problem: "Thanks be to God—through Jesus Christ our Lord!" (Romans 7:25) Paul's mourning could end when he focused on Jesus.

We too should recognize the sin in our lives, mourn over it as God does, and then seek consolation in

Jesus. He Himself promises comfort to those who mourn: "they will be comforted" (Matthew 5:4).

Quiet Strength

Blessed are the meek, for they will inherit the earth.
Matthew 5:5

With the dirt and rust cleaned off, and the primer coat on, the next step in building the bike was to paint that frame a glossy black. Special care was needed at this stage, because the paint job would be evident to all who looked.

What do people see when they look at us? Jesus calls disciples to display a particular attitude. He says, "Blessed are the meek."

Even though the words rhyme, "meek" does not mean "weak." The best proof of this comes from Numbers 12:3, which says that Moses was the meekest, or most humble, man on earth. You remember Moses—the fellow who stood up to the ruler of the world's greatest power, Egypt. Moses brought a scraggly, rebellious, argumentative collection of nomads—the Israelites—under control and led them through the desert for 40 years. Weak? Hardly. Meek? Extremely.

Meekness requires *carefully controlled strength*. Just as a mighty river can be harnessed for a mill or a turbine, so a disciple's strength must be channeled and guided by the Lord. The disciple does not need to flaunt his abilities or prove his prowess. He can rest in Jesus' strength. In the end, the believer

An Acquired Taste

> *Blessed are those who hunger and thirst for righteousness, for they will be filled.*
>
> Matthew 5:6

We have a tradition in our family that each person can select a special birthday meal. For my daughter (who is three), that means macaroni and cheese, with ice cream for dessert. My tastes are a bit more refined: chicken cordon bleu and blueberry cheesecake. She and I have different preferences, but we both get hungry. You know that feeling—it strikes regularly about three times each day. That is, unless you're playing football or on a diet—then it gnaws at you more often.

When Jesus talks about hunger, He's not referring to a condition that can be satisfied by hamburgers or chocolate. Instead, He wants His disciples to develop a craving for righteousness.

"Righteousness" is a big word that basically means obedience to God's instructions. Do you remember Jesus' response to John the Baptist? John was hesitant to baptize the Lord until He said: "It is proper for us to do this to fulfill all righteousness" (3:15). In other words, Jesus wanted to be baptized because that was a part of God's plan. He obeyed God.

Jesus' disciples must also strive for righteousness. The first step is listening to God and wanting to obey

Him. After that, we begin to do what God wants. This starts a cycle of righteousness.

When you're hungry, you eat. But what happens a few hours later? You're hungry again! Is that because you didn't eat enough earlier? Probably not. It happens because hunger is a natural part of the way our bodies work.

When we hunger for righteousness, we will have times of satisfaction. Those times come after you've done something that pleases God—spoken a kind word to a sibling, straightened your room without complaining, shared your faith with a friend. But you don't stop there. These acts should be done more frequently, as righteousness becomes a way of life.

Right now, we have moments of satisfaction when it comes to righteousness—something like the feeling you get when you satisfy your hunger with a turkey dinner. Jesus promises a time when the hunger for righteousness will be satisfied—"they will be filled" (5:6). We'll be completely righteous, and won't hunger anymore. We'll be like Jesus when we are with Him.

Straight from the Heart

Blessed are the merciful, for they will be shown mercy.
Matthew 5:7

Mercy is shown when the sternest neighbor on the block forgives a budding athlete for putting a softball through his living room window. He could justifiably exact a swift penalty, but he shows mercy instead. When Jesus talks about mercy, He wants disciples to consider the mercy they've received from God. Like that neighbor, God could demand total payment for damages. Instead, God offers us forgiveness. He paid the price for our sin with His Son's life. This display of mercy from God should make the disciple eager to show mercy to others.

Jude, a half brother of Jesus (see 13:55), understood mercy. At one point, he and his siblings ignored Jesus, and even thought He was crazy (see Mark 3:21 and John 7:5). Later, something happened to make Jude (along with his brother James) change his mind completely. He became a follower of Jesus.

The little New Testament book he wrote uses the word "mercy" four times. Jude had a special appreciation for God's mercy to him.

Our situation is different from that of Jude—none of us grew up in the same house with Jesus. All the same, God has shown us mercy. Because of this, we must "be merciful to those who doubt . . . [and] to others show mercy" (Jude 22-23). Just as God reached out to forgive us, so we must forgive others, showing mercy—especially to those who don't seem to deserve it.

Refining Fire

Blessed are the pure in heart, for they will see God.
                                        Matthew 5:8

A friend of mine once worked in an aluminum

factory in the Dominican Republic. I visited him one summer and went to see his foundry. A group of men worked there in a small hut, melting down scrap metal. The fire in that hut made the place very hot (it was already over 100° outside!). But without that fire, the scrap metal would never be purified and the new aluminum products would be of poor quality.

Those who would be "pure in heart" must go through a similar refining process. I say "process" because purification takes time. Like metal, we are cleansed by degrees.

This process of purification begins when God turns up the refining fire. Through the Holy Spirit, He begins to show the disciple areas of his life that need changing. If I have a problem with gossiping, I need to have that "burned" away. God wants to help us with this; He wants us to be pure. But we must allow Him to work.

In that aluminum factory, the old cans and engine blocks didn't jump into the fire on their own. A skilled craftsman put them in and then removed the purified metal. Those who are to be purified by God must be willing to let Him work. When that happens, "they will see God."

Middle Ground

Blessed are the peacemakers, for they will be called sons of God.

Matthew 5:9

An argument is like skiing on ice: it's easy to get

started, but difficult to stop.

Jesus addresses the problem of conflict: "Blessed are the peacemakers." Peacemakers may have an opinion, but they don't find it necessary to express themselves at every given opportunity. Instead, peacemakers are interested in forging an agreement between opposing sides.

One of my college professors was an excellent peacemaker. He always seemed able to find good in each side of an argument. He was usually able to work out a compromise that was agreeable to both parties. That way, everyone came out ahead.

Peacemakers, says Jesus, will be called sons of God. This links the peacemaker directly with God. Just as a son displays certain characteristics which are found in his father, so the disciple acts like God in making peace.

And in the End...

> *Blessed are those who are persecuted because of righteousness, for theirs is the kingdom of heaven.*
> Matthew 5:10

We come now to the final Beatitude. The others have been leading up to this point. First, disciples are told what they must get rid of (things like pride in their own abilities) and what they must put on (new appetites and attitudes); now Jesus drops the bombshell.

If the disciple lives the way that Jesus requires, he is going to face trouble. Notice how Jesus puts it:

"Blessed are those who are persecuted because of righteousness." There's that word "righteousness" again; it makes us think about obeying God. The teaching here is that when the disciple lives in obedience to God's instructions, he can expect trouble.

Usually, we think of persecution as torture—something that happened long ago to Christians in Rome, or that happens today in certain countries of the world. But we can broaden the meaning of this word to take in things that all Christians are likely to encounter: loss of popularity, derision, being passed over for a job, and so on. All of these are forms of persecution which can beset those who obviously follow Christ's teachings. Jesus Himself has this in mind when He says: "Blessed are you when people insult you, persecute you and falsely say all kinds of evil against you because of Me" (5:11).

Disciples will face persecution, but when it comes, we are to rejoice (5:12). Why? Because there will be a heavenly reward; those who are persecuted for obeying God and following Christ will receive the kingdom of heaven. The Beatitudes begin and end with God wanting to give us the kingdom of heaven.

It took a lot of work, but George eventually got his bike on the road. The rust was gone; he finally had a beautiful bike whose black paint and silver chrome sparkled in the sun. The effort required had been worthwhile. And for those who ask God to develop in them the attitudes described in Matthew 5:1-12, the rewards will be far greater than they ever imagined.

PRAYER: LEARNING FROM AN EXPERT
Matthew 6:1-13

CHAPTER FOUR

One summer, my brother Paul worked in Detroit for an automobile company. He saw the prototype of a car that the company would eventually sell. This prototype had been built by a group of experts, and it was to serve as the model for other cars that would be produced on an assembly line. Those mass-produced cars would have different colors and accessories, but basically they would follow the general pattern of that one prototype.

In Matthew 6, we find another sort of prototype. It was designed by Jesus, who was an expert in this particular field, and it was intended to serve as a model that His disciples could use for themselves. The model is the "Lord's Prayer," found in verses 9-13.

Often we quote these verses at home or in a church service as an actual prayer. But look at Jesus' words: "This is *how* you should pray" (6:9, italics added). He doesn't say, "This is *what* you should pray." This small difference is important because Jesus is providing His followers with teaching on prayer. He

41

is telling us *how* we should approach God.

If we can think of this portion of the Sermon on the Mount as a set of instructions, then we can learn a great deal about prayer when we look at each separate phrase. Let's do that now, and examine our Lord's Model Prayer.

Our Father

People sometimes think that prayer is too hard, that it requires too much time, or that it is only for religious professionals. Jesus had a very different opinion. For Him, prayer was essential—like sleeping and eating. At times, Jesus made prayer even more important than those things. Matthew remembered that Jesus prayed late into the night (14:23), and Mark knew that He was at prayer early in the morning (Mark 1:35). Both were times when people usually slept.

Jesus prayed for a variety of reasons. One of the most important of these comes out at the start of the Model Prayer: "Our Father." Jesus prayed because it brought Him close to His Father.

Jesus invites His disciples to come to God as their Father. This was a revolutionary idea for a Jew, who viewed God as One who was distant from all but the most extraordinary person. God certainly loved His people, but only special ones like Abraham, Moses, and David enjoyed any sort of close personal relationship with Him. Now, through Jesus, God came very close to people. He could be known, experienced, and loved as a Father. The fancy theological word for this is *imminence*. That word draws attention to the fact that God is close, or imminent.

In prayer, the disciple can call out to Father God, expecting the same sort of kindness and attention any father would give his child. Jesus had already hinted that His disciples could be considered God's children. Remember Matthew 5:9: "Blessed are the peacemakers, for they will be called *sons of God*." Now He makes that relationship crystal clear.

In Heaven

It is true that God is imminent, that He is very near, and that He seeks a close relationship with His children. It is also true that God is distant, or, as theologians say, *transcendent*. He is above all that He has created. This idea shouldn't worry us, nor does it contradict all that we learned from calling God our Father. When Jesus says, "Our Father in heaven," He simply reminds us of another part of God's nature: He is above and beyond all that is. He transcends everything.

The Old Testament writers had a clear understanding of God's transcendence—of His majesty, splendor, and distance from creation. They regularly talked about God dwelling in heaven, a place far removed from this earth. For God to be in heaven was to be superior over all that He had made below. This was an important point to stress among people who too often tended to reduce God's status.

The story of the Tower of Babel is a classic example of people who thought themselves to be nearly equal with God. The result, as we find in Genesis 11, was that God thoroughly confounded their plans to build a structure that reached up to heaven.

Far more appropriate is a stance that shows an awe of God:

> *Do not be quick with your mouth, do not be hasty in your heart to utter anything before God. God is in heaven and you are on earth, so let your words be few.*
> Ecclesiastes 5:2

When disciples approach God through prayer, they draw near to a loving Father. They must also, as Jesus instructs, be aware that the One to whom they are praying is God Almighty, who lives in heaven above.

Hallowed Be Your Name

Prayer properly begins with a recognition of who God is. That is why Jesus encourages His disciples to acknowledge in prayer both the imminence (nearness) and transcendence (distance) of God.

Prayer also includes requests made by the one who is praying. Jesus gives a list of six requests that are appropriate for disciples to bring before God. Three of these deal directly with God Himself, and only after these are dealt with does Jesus allow disciples to present their own needs.

The first thing a disciple should request is that God's name be hallowed: "hallowed be Your name" (6:9). "Hallow" is an old word that comes from "holy." God's name is made holy when God makes those who bear His name holy.

For several years, I worked as a lifeguard at a local YMCA. Every afternoon we closed off a section of the pool so that the local swim team could practice. I watched with fascination as different ones would swim lap after lap. Most of the team did just what was required, but a few would come early and stay late, swimming farther and faster than the rest.

I went to a couple of meets and found that some of the swimmers I knew from the "Y" kept winning their events. It was that same group that put in the extra effort at each practice. They would stand on the winner's podium, proudly wearing their team jackets with the club emblem. They were evidence that the Freeport Aquatics Club produced fine athletes.

Those swimmers brought honor to the name of their club by winning. They won because they were willing to put in the necessary effort.

When we ask God to make His name holy, we—as people who bear His name—must be willing to have Him make us holy. God is already in the process of doing that very thing—we must simply be willing to go along with Him so that we can bring honor and glory to His name.

Your Kingdom Come

Early in His public ministry, Jesus preached about the kingdom of God. He picked up the message of John the Baptist: "Repent, for the kingdom of heaven is near" (Matthew 3:2) and made it His own (see 4:17). Throughout His time on earth, Jesus talked about this kingdom in parables and in public discussion. At times Jesus talked as though the kingdom was present in His day. Other times His words suggested that it was still to come.

Scholars tell us that we should take both of these

conditions as true: the kingdom is both present and future. So when Jesus teaches His followers to ask God to bring on the kingdom—"Your kingdom come"—we should realize that He is after two things.

First, as we pray for the coming of God's kingdom, we are praying for a more complete understanding of Christ for ourselves and those around us. All of us need to know Jesus better, and to have Him influence our lives to a greater extent. This happens as we pray with sincerity.

Second, this part of the prayer reminds us that as Christians, our permanent home is not in this world. We are looking forward to a time when we will be with God. Jesus described that time as the fulfillment of the kingdom—a time when we would together celebrate the great wedding feast of the Lamb (Revelation 19:9). That is the future aspect of the kingdom, and we must remember in our prayers to keep our eyes on that day. The Lord expects us to want to be with Him—and He encourages us to pray for that time to come soon.

Your Will Be Done

The third request also makes the disciple focus on God: "Your will be done on earth as it is in heaven" (Matthew 6:10). God's will is carried out perfectly in heaven; Jesus used this information to encourage disciples to seek the same thing while they are on earth.

How can this be? How can we know the will of God, much less carry it out? It's too vast, too complex.

Or is it?

47 / PRAYER: LEARNING FROM AN EXPERT

We've already seen how, early in His career, Jesus had a clear idea of what God expected from Him. Think back to His baptism, when Jesus acted to "fulfill all righteousness" (3:15). Jesus knew what God wanted, and He did just that; Jesus fulfilled all righteousness by obeying.

In order for God's will to be done on earth, the things that God wants done must be carried out by God's people. It is true that we don't know precisely every single thing that God wants accomplished, but there is a great deal that we do know. Further, it seems reasonable that we should get busy doing what we're sure about, and then wait for God to tell us more.

For example, we do know that God wants us to obey Him through *loving others:* "Dear friends, let us love one another, for love comes from God. Everyone who loves has been born of God and knows God. Whoever does not love does not know God, because God is love" (1 John 4:7-8).

A second way we can obey God is by *being holy,* as He commands: "But just as He who called you is holy, so be holy in all you do; for it is written: 'Be holy, because I am holy' " (1 Peter 1:15-16).

Another of God's desires for each of His disciples is that we *be godly*. Paul talked about this in a letter to Timothy: "Train yourself to be godly. For physical training is of some value, but godliness has value for all things, holding promise for both the present life and the life to come" (1 Timothy 4:7-8).

Once we're in the swing of obeying God through loving others, being holy, and living a consistent godly life, we'll be ready for more. The rest will fall into place.

Give Us Today Our Daily Bread

Not until halfway into the Model Prayer does Jesus tell His disciples to approach God with personal needs. Do you follow this pattern in your own prayers? I know that for me, it is far too easy to sit down to pray and then reel off a bunch of things which concern me: "God, I need this, do that for me, help me here, and P.S.—I love You."

It's far better to open prayer with adoration of God. We should request the hallowing of His name, the bringing on of His kingdom, and the performance of His will before we turn to matters that relate to us. And even when we're ready for that part of the prayer, we must be careful how we proceed.

Jesus puts two significant words in the next phrase: "today" and "bread." He knew the tendency people have to hoard things and to live in the past or the future, rather than in the present. That's why He emphasized the immediate need; disciples are to pray for what they need today: "Give us today our daily bread" (Matthew 6:11).

Another common problem for human nature is to want too much. So Jesus instructs His followers to pray for bread, not cake. Bread is sufficient for sustaining life, and it remains the staple food in much of the world today. Jesus wanted to teach that God is not in the business of handing out credit cards and luxury vacations to His friends. One thing that is certain is God's love—that's never-ending.

49 / PRAYER: LEARNING FROM AN EXPERT

Jesus challenges us to trust God for all our needs. Many have taken His words here to heart and lived by them. One outstanding example of this is George Mueller, who ran an orphanage in England in the 19th century. At times he would call the children to a meal, even though the pantry was empty. Together they would give thanks for God's provision. With the final amen, a knock would come at the door. Outside would be a truck driver, wondering whether the orphanage could use some day-old bakery goods.

Forgive Us as We Forgive

God promises to forgive the sins of every person who accepts His Son as Saviour and Lord. We can rest secure in this promise. At the same time, we must realize that our daily lives still contain sin because of the wrong choices we make. The presence of sin in our lives impairs our relationship with God. That's why Jesus wants His disciples to ask God's forgiveness regularly in prayer.

Jesus also has another thought in mind when He includes this line in His Model Prayer. He wants His followers to remember how much God has already forgiven them, and how this in turn should affect their relationships with those who need their forgiveness. He says, "Forgive us our debts, as we also have forgiven our debtors" (6:12).

One time Jesus told the story of a man whose king forgave him of a tremendous debt. When the man refused to forgive another person of a much smaller charge, the king tossed the first one into prison (18:23-35). He had not learned the lesson the king tried to teach: forgiveness should inspire forgiveness. Similarly, disciples of Christ need to realize how much God has forgiven them, and be ready and willing to forgive when others wrong them.

Lead Us, Deliver Us

Jesus' Model Prayer concludes with one last request. Like the ones for bread and forgiveness, this last entreaty brings out the disciple's need for God in daily life. Food and forgiveness are just as important as protection from Satan.

Each of the New Testament writers takes seriously the existence of beings that are not immediately visible to us. Paul's expression is probably the best known:

> *Our struggle is not against flesh and blood, but against the rulers, against the authorities, against the powers of this dark world and against the spiritual forces of evil in the heavenly realms.*
>
> Ephesians 6:12

Jesus had already faced Satan in the wilderness. He knew how crafty the evil one could be. So He knew how much His disciples needed God's protection.

Peter compared the devil to a roaring lion that prowls around "looking for someone to devour" (1 Peter 5:8). We cannot afford to treat the evil one like a tame kitten that simply hisses once in a while. Christ's disciples need instead to be on their guard, praying specifically and often for deliverance from the enemy's snares: "And lead us not into temptation, but deliver us from the evil one" (Matthew 6:13).

Amen

Like that prototype automobile in Detroit, the Lord's Model Prayer was formulated to give us an idea of what our prayers should be like. Jesus carefully points out three important elements of prayer:

- Adoration of God's person.
- Expectation of God's glorification.
- Anticipation of God's provision.

We could look elsewhere in Scripture for other principles of prayer, but these are enough to get us started. God expects us to pray, as Jesus shows by saying "when you pray" (6:5-7).

Prayer brings us right up alongside God. When we pray, we come into His presence; and He prepares us to live a life which brings Him glory. This is the lesson the disciple must learn: following Christ means getting to know God even as Christ knew Him. Prayer is an essential part of knowing God.

HITTING THE ROAD
Matthew 6:19–7:23

CHAPTER FIVE

We've looked at the Beatitudes and examined Jesus' Model Prayer, but there is still more of the Sermon on the Mount to explore. Jesus gives His disciples instructions that will help them on their way. It's almost as though He is acting as a tour guide, advising the disciples about a particular trip. The trip is the process of discipleship, and the Leader gives principles as a map to follow.

Plotting the Course

What is the longest trip you've ever taken? Mine was a family vacation I took as a child which led through several Western states to a camp in California. This was new territory to kids who were then living in the Midwest, so my parents suggested that we read up on the area. That started us sifting through old *National Geographic* magazines and checking books out of the library.

After a few weeks of this, we began to plan the details of our trip. We wrote to different state tourism offices and watched a pile of brochures grow on our dining room table. Each night we'd sit down and look for an interesting town or attraction to visit.

Finally, the time came to leave. We flew first to Las Vegas to pick up a car. Then we loaded all our carefully selected gear—cameras, maps, frisbees, etc. At last we were off.

The Nevada desert was hotter than we had imagined. When the car wasn't boiling over, someone's temper was. We quickly learned that the success of our trip required patience, calmness, and enthusiasm from everyone in the car.

This last part of Jesus' long Sermon on the Mount describes a trip something like our family vacation years ago. On any trip, both the travel and the destination are important; Jesus talks about both. He gives advice on "The Plans to Make," "Some Things Not to Take," and "Some Habits to Break." Then He warns us to "Watch Out for Fakes."

The Plans to Make

When it came time to plot our trip West, we sat down with an atlas, a stack of brochures, and unlimited imagination. It was only when my parents added their comments that we saw what was realistic and what was not. They had been this way before—they knew what we would enjoy and what we could afford.

In the same way, Jesus' advice is valuable because He knows about both the journey and the destination. He has experienced the sorts of trials His disciples will encounter, and He knows what joys and frustrations they will face.

One of the tendencies on any trip is to try to do too much. When we were planning ours, we thought, *As long as we're driving through Nevada, Arizona, Colorado, and California, why not take in Texas, Oklahoma, New Mexico, and Utah?* Fortunately, Dad quickly decided that such an attempt was out of the question. It would spread us too thin and detract from our main purpose of seeing and enjoying just a few special sites.

Jesus knows about this tendency. That's why He encourages His followers to be single-minded. They are not to wander aimlessly, but proceed carefully toward their destination. Jesus told His disciples, "Be perfect, therefore, as your Heavenly Father is perfect" (Matthew 5:48). This provides a guideline for the trip: they are to be like God as they go.

Being like God affects every part of the disciple's life. It means wanting what God wants, seeing things as God sees them, reaching out to help those who have needs. With that sort of mindset, the trip can begin.

Some Things Not to Take

To help us know what to pack, Jesus gives luggage restrictions for this trip:

> *Do not store up for yourselves treasures on earth, where moth and rust destroy, and where thieves break in and steal. But store up for yourselves treasures in heaven, where moth and rust do not destroy, and where thieves do not break in and steal. For where your treasure is, there your heart will be also.*
>
> Matthew 6:19-21

Jesus wants disciples to travel light, taking nothing that would impede progress. You can't do both. The Apostle Paul put it this way: "Set your hearts on things above, where Christ is seated at the right hand of God. Set your minds on things above, not on earthly things" (Colossians 3:1-2). Paul expects disciples to be consumed with the things of God.

Jesus knows about the tendency to pack too much, which means wasting space with things you don't need. I've learned this too, now that I have a family which includes two small girls. When we load the car for a jaunt to the lake, it looks as though we're prepared for a journey around the world. Inevitably, we use only a fraction of the books, toys, and food that we bring.

Not only is there an urge to pack too much, but there is also the tendency to bring the wrong stuff. Jesus points out that the material things we value, the things we might want to take with us on a long trip, are ultimately of little use. According to Jesus, the possessions we prize so highly are enticements to robbers. They are prone to natural erosion, and they serve as taste treats for insects. Seen in this light, it is no wonder that Jesus wants disciples to bring along what is of more permanent value—"treasures in heaven."

How do we attain these treasures? We need to have hearts and minds that are tuned to things above—heavenly things. We should be interested in cultivating and demonstrating the fruit of the Spirit: "love, joy, peace, patience, kindness, goodness, faithfulness, gentleness and self-control" (Galatians 5:22). These qualities will produce works that have eternal value, and cannot be stolen by thieves on earth or destroyed by rust or moths. The deeds that result from hearts set on God will have eternal value. They are treasures that will last forever in heaven.

What we value makes a statement about who we are. What kind of things do you take to the beach or the mountains when you go on vacation? Don't the clothes, stereo, and sporting gear all say something about who you are and what you think is important?

Disciples who cultivate treasures in heaven show that their hearts are also in heaven. Think of it in this way: you can choose the sort of influences which will govern your life. You can be controlled by a desire to please God and be more like Christ. Or you can be weighed down with earthly things that fade away. Which of these options implies a heart set on heavenly treasure? Which is appropriate for the trip Jesus describes?

You'll notice that Jesus says very little about the *material* things that we take with us. In fact, He seems to suggest that *things* will only rust and spoil. Much more important is a disciple's *attitude*. A person who focuses on God stores up treasures in heaven. Just as a hiker on the Appalachian Trail will leave the Twinkies at home to make room for a sleeping bag and beef jerky, a follower of Christ must also learn to take along what is of real value in the spiritual realm.

Some Habits to Break

Driving through Death Valley while sitting in the last backseat of a station wagon, wedged in among suitcases, was not fun. I was already prone to complain, and this experience simply brought out the worst in me. I learned, though, that my complaints did little to make the time pass more quickly, the seat grow softer, or the outside air become cooler. In fact, they only made the other passengers more irritable. Finally, my folks took the matter in hand. During one of our frequent "radiator stops," they persuaded me to modify my behavior and attitude. Or else! I took their advice, and gradually noticed an improvement. The outside air was still hot and the seat was still sticky and uncomfortable, but the travelers were less moody. I got to the point where I actually enjoyed (well, almost enjoyed) watching cactus fly by.

Any disciple who takes the trip Jesus has laid out will find it necessary to change behavior patterns. Annoying habits wear down fellow travelers. Not only that, but some behavior is downright sinful.

Jesus mentions two problems in particular. The first deals with a common difficulty—worry. Jesus' words, taken at face value, seem almost too good to be true:

> *Do not worry about your life, what you will eat or drink; or about your body, what you will wear. Is not life more important than food, and the body more important than clothes? Look at the birds of the air; they do not sow or reap or store away in barns, and yet your heavenly Father feeds them. Are you not much more valuable than they? Who of you by worrying can add a single hour to his life?*
>
> Matthew 6:25-27

Jesus was talking to a group of people who quite

naturally were prone to worry. He tried to convince them that God's provision would overcome any deficiency they might encounter. In the end, Jesus' first disciples learned this lesson, and in the Book of Acts we see disciples who are empowered by the Spirit and have left their worries behind.

The second point that Jesus addressed was the tendency to criticize:

> *Do not judge, or you too will be judged. For in the same way you judge others, you will be judged, and with the measure you use, it will be measured to you.*
> Matthew 7:1-2

This was a serious problem in Jesus' day, and it remains serious for us. How often have you gone through an entire day without criticizing someone? It's easy to have a critical spirit, but Jesus warns against it.

Both of these problems make me take my eyes off God and start looking at myself. When I worry, I show my fear that God really won't care for my needs. When I criticize, I put someone else down, usually so I can look good by comparison.

Jesus condemns both errors. His directions are very clear: do not worry, and do not judge. Both of these become problems of habit—we start to worry and then remain anxious. Or we begin with one small "harmless" criticism, and then find that we are soon looking down our noses at everything a person does.

For our trip to be successful, we must change some of these bad habits. Jesus' advice is to consider lilies of the field which do not work, yet still wear beautiful clothes (6:28-29). So why worry?

He also encourages a perspective which focuses not on the shortcomings of others, but on our own deficiencies.

> *Why do you look at the speck of sawdust in your brother's eye and pay no attention to the plank in your own eye? You hypocrite, first take the plank out of your own eye, and then you will see clearly to remove the speck from your brother's eye.*
>
> Matthew 7:3, 5

Once we begin to develop the right habits, we can make real progress on our trip. But there is still one last piece of advice that Jesus gives His disciples.

Watch Out for Fakes

On your last road trip you may have noticed many billboards advertising all sorts of wonderful promises. This phenomenon is especially apparent as you approach a "tourist trap." Have you ever pulled into a cafe that claimed to have "The World's Best Chili," but didn't? How about a motel with a swimming pool that was more like a birdbath? On our trip West, we found a number of billboards that were, to put it nicely, optimistic.

We really shouldn't have been surprised. Why wouldn't a merchant want to put his best foot forward? The problem is that claims do not always stop at "optimistic." P.T. Barnum, that great originator of spectacular circuses, observed that "there's a sucker born every minute," and it seems like some are out to prove him right! People are easily fooled.

Jesus warned His followers that they would encounter people like this along the way. He didn't want them to suspect every person they met of being a fraud, but He did offer some helpful criteria:

> *Watch out for false prophets. They come to you in sheep's clothing, but inwardly they are ferocious wolves. By their fruit you will recognize them. Do people pick grapes from thornbushes, or figs from thistles? Likewise every good tree bears good fruit, but a bad tree bears bad fruit. A good tree cannot bear bad fruit, and a bad tree cannot bear good fruit.*
>
> Matthew 7:15-18

At first glance, it looks as if this passage contradicts what Jesus said earlier about not judging. But let's look at these words more closely.

First, Jesus encourages His followers not to be critical and negative when dealing with other people. He wants disciples to lift others up, not put them down (7:1-5).

Later, Jesus addresses the problems that arise when people make certain claims about themselves that are not true. He tells His disciples they must examine the "fruit" these people bear (7:15-20).

In the first case, Jesus wants disciples to look at themselves and deal with problems of criticism and selfishness. In the second, He wants them to guard against those who try to mislead them.

Jesus gives a principle: all who claim to be disciples must exhibit certain characteristics in their lives. If these characteristics are missing from one who claims to be a follower, then other followers are to beware. "By their fruit you will recognize them" (7:20).

Jesus expects disciples to bear "fruit." In other words, there should be evidence of the presence of God in a person's life. This "fruit" includes, as we've already seen, things like love, joy, peace, and kindness (Galatians 5:22). If these are missing from one who claims to be a follower, then some sort of deceit is taking place. Deeds that a true follower does can also be examples of good fruit.

When it comes to judging ourselves, we are to be very strict. But when it comes to judging others, we are to give them every opportunity to prove themselves honest. However, since some people are deceitful, Jesus includes warnings and instructions about how to evaluate the claims of another. If the "fruit" is bad, disciples must be on their guard.

Peter warns that "your enemy the devil prowls around like a roaring lion looking for someone to devour" (1 Peter 5:8). We must realize that the evil one is looking for ways to deceive and devour those who love God. And we must take care that we do not fall prey to his traps.

End of the Line

Most of the comments we've read have dealt with the journey itself—the process of discipleship. Jesus tells disciples just how they are to act if they want to have a profitable travel experience.

But Jesus is also interested in the final destination. The journey is important, both in itself and also because of where it takes us—into God's very presence. At the end of His Sermon on the Mount, Jesus talks about entering the kingdom of heaven (Matthew 7:13-14, 21-23).

> *Enter through the narrow gate. For wide is the gate and broad is the road that leads to destruction, and many enter through it. But small is the gate and narrow the road that leads to life, and only a few find it.*
>
> Matthew 7:13-14

Not many travelers find the right road, Jesus says. But for those who decide to follow the Leader down the narrow road, reaching the final destination will be worth the discipline of the trip.

We enjoyed (finally) our trip in the car. The Grand Canyon and the Mojave Desert were definitely worth seeing. The best part, though, was driving into a camp in northern California to spend a week in one place.

The disciple's journey takes a lifetime, and it involves a variety of experiences. But the best part by far will be to reach the end of "the road that leads to life," and remain forever with God.

IT'S A MIRACLE!
Matthew 8–9

CHAPTER SIX

We've seen that Jesus is a Leader worth following and a teacher interested in developing His disciples. Now we're going to find that this disciple-maker is also a miracle worker.

I hope you've been reading through Matthew's Gospel as we've gone along in this study. Before you go any further, take five minutes to scan the contents of Matthew 8 and 9. This will help you understand better some of the things I'll talk about in this chapter.

Did you notice the many miracles that Matthew records in these two chapters? In fact, he writes about little else. Since all the Gospel writers stress the place of miracles in Jesus' ministry, we should make sure we understand the basics about them.

Signs of the Times

Wonder-workers were common during the first century A.D. The Book of Acts, for example, tells stories about fortune-tellers (16:16-21) and sorcerers (8:9-25). So when Jesus came along, some of the things He did weren't unusual by comparison.

Jesus came into a culture that knew firsthand about magic. Because of that, He took special care to ensure that His miracles weren't misinterpreted as bids for recognition, or the work of one possessed by the devil. Jesus regularly attributed His power for performing miracles to God.

Two other aspects of Jesus' miracles set them apart from the tricks done by crowd-seekers: Jesus' miracles genuinely helped people, and they showed His relationship to God.

Both of these points are important. Other wonder-workers were usually looking out for their own welfare. The sorcerer mentioned in Acts 8 saw ways to turn a profit using unusual abilities. Jesus had completely different intentions with His miracles.

It doesn't take too long to think of a miracle that Jesus did to help someone. Such acts range from the quieting of a raging storm which had terrified frightened disciples (Mark 4:35-41) to the feeding of a crowd of hungry people (Luke 9:10-17). Most often, Jesus' miracles helped sick people by healing them.

Miracles also established Jesus' relationship with God. Jesus Himself made this clear: "I tell you the truth, the Son can do nothing by Himself; He can do only what He sees His Father doing, because whatever the Father does the Son also does" (John 5:19). Jesus relied on God when He performed miracles.

Matthew 8 and 9 record Jesus helping 11 different people. Most of these were sick, so we should investigate why Jesus was so interested in healing. To do

this, let's consider three points:
- The importance of believing in Jesus.
- Jesus' willingness to minister to all kinds of people.
- The tie between physical and spiritual health.

Faith

Faith plays a part in virtually every miracle described in the Gospels. In the Synoptic Gospels (Matthew, Mark, and Luke), the pattern is usually that a person with faith approaches Jesus and is then helped by Him. John suggests that Jesus' miracles actually produced or strengthened faith in people. But all four writers agree that there is a strong connection between faith and miracles.

Look at the miracles recounted in Matthew 8 and 9, and notice how often faith is mentioned:

"Lord, if You are willing, You can make me clean" (8:2). The leper believed that Jesus could help him.

"I tell you the truth, I have not found anyone in Israel with such great faith" (8:10). The centurion whose servant was sick exhibited remarkable faith.

"Some men brought to Him a paralytic, lying on a mat. When Jesus saw their faith, He said to the paralytic, 'Take heart, son; your sins are forgiven'" (9:2). The paralytic's friends had faith to bring the man to Jesus.

"'Take heart, daughter,' He said, 'your faith has

healed you' " (9:22). The woman who was subject to bleeding demonstrated faith by touching Jesus.

" 'Do you believe I am able to do this?' 'Yes, Lord,' they replied" (9:28). Two blind men called out to Jesus in faith.

These are five examples of people who were healed because of belief in Jesus' ability to heal. Their faith was not random or general—they didn't simply believe that anyone and everyone could heal them. Rather, they sought Jesus and were rewarded for trusting Him.

Have you noticed how their faith was expressed? Each one showed his faith by *doing* something:

A man with leprosy came and knelt before Jesus.

A centurion came to Jesus.

Some men brought a paralytic to Jesus.

A woman came up behind Jesus and touched the edge of His cloak.

Two blind men followed Jesus and called out to Him.

All of these situations point out what the New Testament teaches us about faith:

Faith = Belief + Action

These people all believed that Jesus could do something about their problems, and they all took action which demonstrated their belief. Their faith was then rewarded.

The flip side to miracles is given later. Matthew tells us that when Jesus went to His hometown of

Nazareth, He did not do many miracles because faith was not evident in the people there (13:53-58). The appropriate context for the performance of a miracle was missing: the people of Nazareth did not demonstrate the faith which others had already shown.

Favoritism

Another point which comes out as we study Jesus' miracles is His complete lack of favoritism. Jesus was interested in all sorts of people and needs:

1. A leper (8:2-4). Because lepers had a skin disease thought to be contagious, they were required to live quarantined by themselves in a community outside the city limits. When Jesus "reached out His hand and touched the man" (8:3), He showed no fear of a dreaded disease; He broke through a large social barrier. Jesus' compassion, so often evident in His healing touch, transcended customs and status. He ministered to need wherever He found it.

2. A centurion (8:5-13). Only Roman citizens could be centurions. Not only was the man Jesus spoke with a Gentile (and therefore off-limits for a pious Jew), but he was also a Roman—particularly despised in Israel. Jesus' willingness to help this man and heal his servant cut across another social barrier; it might even have led some to think of Jesus as a traitor who was giving aid and comfort to the enemy.

3. Two demoniacs (8:28-34). Both Mark (5:1-20) and Luke (8:26-39) know about this story, but they each report on only one demoniac. Since neither one insists that only one was healed, there is no immediate reason to think that Matthew is either confused or wrong. The main point of this episode is that again Jesus reached out to men who had been abandoned by others. Not only that, but Jesus encountered the men He healed in or near a graveyard. This sort of place was totally off-limits to religious Jews, and so Jesus' work with the demoniacs is doubly significant: He went into a place which was judged to be inappropriate, and He healed people who had been given up by others.

4. *A woman* (9:20-22). In Jesus' day, women were treated like possessions which could be acquired and discarded rather easily. They had virtually no rights of their own, and they were rarely regarded favorably. Jesus regularly opposed these cultural standards, and He showed respect for women as part of God's creation.

In this episode, Jesus was on His way to go to the home of a synagogue ruler whose daughter was ill when He stopped to talk with a woman who had been hemorrhaging for 12 years. Mark (5:35) says that it was during this delay that the ruler's daughter died; but Jesus thought the need of the bleeding woman warranted immediate attention. Again He cut across what was socially accepted (going to help a prominent member of the community) to meet a particular need (healing a chronically ill woman). Then He went to the ruler's house and raised his daughter from the dead.

Fitness

So far, we've talked about the faith present in people whom Jesus healed, and we've considered the significance of Jesus' choices to heal these particular people. Now we should pause for a bit to think about the miracles themselves. After all, why *did* Jesus perform miracles? I've already suggested that He did this for two reasons: to help people and to show His relationship with God. There was also a third reason: by healing bodies, Jesus showed His interest in saving souls.

Maybe that reason sounds a bit strange, so let me explain myself. Originally, the New Testament was written in Greek, and it has since been translated into modern languages, such as English. In Greek, the word which describes healing is the same one translated into English as "salvation." In other words, healing and saving are really the same idea, but in English they are talked about in different ways.

Jesus came to earth to save souls. He did this by offering forgiveness to people. At the same time, many of those who needed saving also had urgent physical needs: they were blind, deaf, and paralyzed.

It was certainly true that people who were healthy also needed to be saved from their sins. Jesus did not ignore this fact; He offered salvation to all who asked.

As God's Son, Jesus reached into people's souls to save them—to heal them spiritually. His miracles of physical healing gave a tangible sign of what was an accomplished spiritual reality.

Finale

What do we learn from this lesson on miracles? One thing we ought to notice immediately is Jesus' attitude. He didn't perform miracles just to grab attention or to show off. Many times, He actually disappeared immediately after doing a miracle, or He would urge a healed person to remain silent about what He had done.

Jesus responded to faith. He was willing to work in the life of someone who trusted His ability to heal. Second, Jesus' miracles show us that He never played favorites. Jesus was interested in all sorts of people, and He was eager to help them all. Can you imagine reaching out to the guy who lives in the computer room at school, the football jock, or the girl who sits in the cafeteria eating her way into oblivion? Those are the kinds of people Jesus talked with, ate with, touched.

Finally, Jesus taught that there is a connection between a person's body and soul. That means that we can't just try to witness to someone on a spiritual level—we must also be willing to meet physical needs.

One of the strongest childhood memories I have is of going to church in downtown Pittsburgh at Christmastime to fill up baskets of groceries. The baskets were then distributed to people who needed food. At the time, I really didn't understand what we were doing, but I can remember being in that big room with lots of smiling people. They were happy to be doing that work! Those folks had the right idea: they were trying to meet real physical needs in the neighborhood around them.

Since then, I've been with other groups that have done similar things at Christmas or Thanksgiving. And I've learned that when Christians reach out, others become more receptive to hearing the Gospel.

Jesus values the soul, and He also showed that a

person's body is important. His miracles of healing were more dramatic than what most of us will see done, or do ourselves. But we can still have the same concern for people that Jesus had—a concern that wants to see people whole, healthy, and saved.

FLYING LESSONS
Matthew 10:1–11:7

CHAPTER SEVEN

My brother and I had a variety of ways to earn spending money while we were growing up. We both delivered newspapers, sold golf balls fished out of water hazards, and worked at summer camp. Eventually we hit upon one scheme that really paid off: washing and waxing small private airplanes.

We started hanging around the airport, trying to drum up business. I remember sitting in the small office there, reading the bulletin boards that advertised flying lessons. Part of me thought that flying would be fun, but part of me (the larger part) was hesitant—too much time, too much money, too much risk.

I decided instead to stay on the ground. I could wash and wax planes, get a vicarious thrill watching them take off and land, and then go home, with bank account and body still intact. I learned a lot about flying. The only drawback was that I never got to see our tiny island in the Bahamas from the cockpit of a four-seater.

The Disciples in Flight Training

In Matthew 10, we are introduced to 12 men who took up their own kind of flying lessons and then went on to be pilots themselves. These men were Jesus' closest disciples, who lived with Him during the three years of His public ministry.

The list Matthew gives is similar to the ones in Mark and Luke, with just a few differences. Look at this table and see if you can pick out the variations:

Matthew 10:2-4	Mark 3:16-18	Luke 6:14-16
Simon (called Peter)	Simon (called Peter)	Simon (called Peter)
Andrew (Simon's brother)	James (son of Zebedee)	Andrew (Simon's brother)
James (son of Zebedee)	John (James' brother)	James
John (James' brother)	Andrew	John
Philip	Philip	Philip
Bartholomew	Bartholomew	Bartholomew
Thomas	Matthew	Matthew
Matthew (the tax collector)	Thomas	Thomas
James (son of Alphaeus)	James (son of Alphaeus)	James (son of Alphaeus)
Thaddaeus	Thaddaeus	Simon (the Zealot)
Simon (the Zealot)	Simon (the Zealot)	Judas (son of James)
Judas Iscariot	Judas Iscariot	Judas Iscariot

There are two kinds of differences in these lists.

74 / FOLLOW THE LEADER

One is a difference in order, and the other is a difference in actual names.

The differences in order aren't too important. The early lists of names that would have circulated among the first-century churches were probably kept in six pairs; switching the order of the pairs (like Matthew and Thomas) didn't mean much.

Differences in actual names aren't too important either, but they are interesting for us to see. People in Bible times often had more than one name. For example, Joseph of Cyprus was called Barnabas (Acts 4:36). Dorcas, a Greek name, was called Tabitha in Aramaic (Acts 9:36). Simon's second name, Peter, is hardly thought of because it is used so frequently in the New Testament.

It shouldn't surprise us, then, that other disciples had more than one name. This is true for the son of James known as both Thaddaeus and Judas. This Judas probably took on another name to distinguish himself from Judas Iscariot. Though it is not evident in the Synoptic Gospels, it appears that Bartholomew also had a second name. John knows him as Nathanael (John 1:45; 21:2).

To complete the matter, we probably ought to note that at least three of the Twelve had nicknames. Thomas was called Didymus, which means "twin" (John 20:24-28).

Jesus named James and John Boanerges, which means Sons of Thunder (Mark 3:17).

Apart from their names, we have a little information about some of the disciples:

1. At least four of them were fishermen by trade (Peter, Andrew, James, and John).

2. One of them worked, for a while at least, for the Roman government (Matthew, the tax collector).
3. The group had at least two sets of brothers (Simon and Andrew, James and John). It may be that there was another set of brothers. Mark calls Matthew (or Levi) a son of Alphaeus (Mark 2:14). James, another disciple, was also the son of a man named Alphaeus. If this was the same Alphaeus, then Matthew and this James were also brothers.
4. One of them was a political activist (Simon the Zealot).

Servant Attitudes

Does this give you a better feel for Jesus' 12 closest followers? Does it seem like an unlikely set of people to you?

If we were to look outside the New Testament, into the records of church history, we would find a few more details about their lives. There are also a great many legends about what they did after Jesus returned to heaven. But these stories, while fun to read, aren't very reliable.

It is a little surprising that the New Testament itself doesn't tell us more about their lives. After all, they spent three intense years with Jesus, and were highly revered by fellow Christians. These men were responsible for much of the growth in the early church.

There may be little information available because these men themselves made a conscious effort not to have their stories blown out of proportion. By the time Jesus returned to heaven, they had learned one of His lessons the hard way: "Whoever wants to become great among you must be your servant, and whoever wants to be first must be slave of all" (Mark 10:43-44). They saw Jesus, the Suffering Servant, die.

For the Twelve, serving God was much more important than being famous. Instead of placing them on a pedestal, the early church preferred instead to remember and follow the message the disciples brought—the words they had learned from Jesus.

Your Mission, Should You Choose to Accept It...

You may remember or may have seen reruns of the old TV show "Mission: Impossible." It always began with a tape-recorded message inviting Jim Phelps to turn down an incredibly difficult task. Of course, he never did. He simply picked out his team and then carefully executed his assignment.

Jesus also picked out His team. Then He sent them out to do a job. He told them where to go, what to say, and how to act.

> *Do not go among the Gentiles or enter any town of the Samaritans. Go rather to the lost sheep of Israel. As you go, preach this message: "The kingdom of heaven is near." Heal the sick, raise the dead, cleanse those who have leprosy, drive out demons. Freely you have received, freely give.*
>
> Matthew 10:5-8

The disciples had been following Jesus for some

time. Just as my brother and I learned about flying by hanging around that airport, these men had been soaking up lessons from Jesus. Then He told them they were ready to solo.

Their first mission took them over Jewish territory. Later, Jesus expanded the scope of the disciples' ministry. But He wanted them first to concentrate on an area that was more familiar. This was a good way of building their confidence, having them test their skills with the minimum risk. It was a little like a junior pilot sitting in a flight simulator, having to go through all the activity required by a flight.

Once He had told them where to go, Jesus told the disciples what to say when they got there. The message was simple: "The kingdom of heaven is near" (10:7). That was virtually the same pronouncement that Jesus made when He began to preach (see 4:17). The disciples were to continue announcing to those living in Israel the reality and presence of God's kingdom.

What exactly is this kingdom? Why did Jesus talk so much about it?

Put simply, the kingdom of heaven is the sphere in which God works. He sent His Son to perform miracles, and He enabled the subjects of the kingdom (that is, followers of Jesus) to live in a particular way—according to the precepts laid out in the Sermon on the Mount, for instance. (This kingdom is also called the kingdom of God.) Today's followers of Jesus are part of the kingdom of heaven too.

With the destination and the message in mind, the disciples were ready for some advice about their demeanor. Jesus told them how to act:

Do not take along any gold or silver or copper in your belts; take no bag for the journey, or extra tunic, or sandals or a staff; for the worker is worth his keep.
Matthew 10:9-10

The disciples were going on a brief but urgent mission. They were to take no suitcase or credit card; they would go out in God's power alone. They were commissioned to heal and restore broken people, and they were to rely on others for the necessities of life, like room and board.

These instructions were geared to test the disciples; performing miracles and relying on other people both required faith. Jesus wanted His followers to trust in God for the mundane as well as the supernatural.

The disciples were to act decisively. Jesus expected them to determine whether people were sufficiently responsive to their message. If given a warm welcome, they were to stay—preaching, teaching, and healing. But if the townspeople rejected them, as they had occasionally rejected Jesus (e.g., see Mark 5:17), then the disciples were to move on. Not even the dust from the roads of that town was to cling to their feet.

Part of decisive action was discerning the character of other people. When Jesus instructed His followers to "be as shrewd as snakes and as innocent as doves" (Matthew 10:16), He was warning them about the nature of those they would encounter. He wanted them to avoid foolish risk. At the same time, Jesus knew that His message would disturb people and that it might result in trouble for His disciples. That is why He promised that God would help them should negative circumstances arise (10:18-20).

79 / FLYING LESSONS

A disciple cannot be merely a passive follower. He must also be an active proclaimer. Such proclamation will have tremendous results for good at times. There are examples of this in the Old Testament, such as the ministries of Jonah and Haggai. At other times, the outcome will be disastrous. Matthew describes this sort of situation in his next chapter.

What Do You Expect?

John, who was famous for baptizing people, was in jail. He had been put there by evil King Herod because he refused to tone down his strong message. Part of that message condemned Herod for his sinful lifestyle. Eventually, John was killed for his high principles.

While John was in prison, he had time to think. He reflected on his years of contemplation and preparation in the desert, on his sudden rise to prominence in Israel, and on the crashing fall his imprisonment brought. No doubt he thought occasionally of the fate that awaited most of Herod's prisoners—death.

John also would have thought about Jesus. Perhaps he got to wondering whether he'd done the right thing. Did he deserve to be in jail? Wasn't he too young to die? Was Jesus really the One he had anticipated, the Saviour of Israel?

Finally, John sent one of his own followers to Jesus to ask: "Are You the One who was to come, or should we expect someone else?" (11:3)

John's problem was a common one: his expectations had not been fulfilled. Like most of the Jews around him, John was expecting a Messiah to come who would act as a triumphant king, one who would throw the Romans out of Israel and put Jewish leaders in their place.

Jesus, heralded by John as the One sent by God (see John 1:29-34), did not measure up to what others wanted. He was meek and humble, not brash and swaggering. He avoided opportunities to set up a political kingdom (see John 6:15). He gave no fiery speeches. This was most peculiar for one who was supposed to be a great king.

What was John to think?

A friend once taught me a valuable lesson about expectations. He likened them to puffs of air going into a balloon, which grew larger and larger until the balloon finally burst. The flimsy rubber simply couldn't contain all that was pumped into it.

The lesson was clear to me. When we start building up expectations, they too quickly get away from us. Pretty soon they are out of control and threaten to ruin things entirely. Stop for a moment and think: what kinds of expectations do you build up? Maybe that your parents will always be right. Or that every single detail of your first date will be perfect. Or that your grades and test scores will be high enough to launch a fabulous career.

By this point, you probably already know that life can deal out a lot of disappointments. Have you stopped to consider why this is? Do disappointments sometimes come because you wanted too much— because your expectations were unrealistic? Did you try to put too much air in the balloon?

Jesus knew the problems with expectations, so He could understand the questions that John sent. And because He knew human nature so well, Jesus could answer those questions in a way that helped reshape John's expectations:

> *Go back and report to John what you hear and see: The blind receive sight, the lame walk, those who have leprosy are cured, the deaf hear, the dead are raised, and the good news is preached to the poor.*
> Matthew 11:4-5

Jesus told the messengers from John: "Look, I'm doing the things the Saviour is supposed to do. These things alone should prove that I am the One you expected" (see Isaiah 35:5-6; 61:1-2). On top of this, Jesus added, "Blessed is the man who does not fall away on account of Me" (Matthew 11:6).

Jesus knew that people were looking for a king to come and save them from all their troubles; He knew that they had filled their balloons almost to the bursting point. His comments to John were designed to let some of the air out, to change expectations so that John and others could accept Jesus as He was. Jesus *was* the Messiah, but not the sort of Messiah everyone was looking for. He first had to go through some hard times that would be difficult for them to understand if they didn't modify their hopes. There would be a period of victory and triumph for the Messiah, but that was still in the future.

John learned this lesson. He did not lose faith in Jesus. Because of his questions and Jesus' response, we can learn the need to have our own expectations modified by what God wants. As Jesus said another time, "The work of God is this: to believe in the One

He has sent" (John 6:29). In other words, we must listen to God as He spoke through His Son, and take care that our expectations do not become unrealistic.

John the Baptist was not merely content to sit around the hangar and watch others learn to fly. He walked out and signed up for lessons. Then he climbed in behind the instruments and took off down the runway. There were a few anxious moments mid-air; but after a while—like Peter, Andrew, James, and John—he could solo.

THE POINT OF PARABLES
Matthew 13:1-45

CHAPTER EIGHT

Now that we have two kids, my wife and I are thinking more seriously about family traditions. One event that is fast on its way to becoming a regular part of our lives is the Sunday Morning Donut and Paper Run. This begins sometime between 6:30 and 7:00 A.M., when one of the girls wakes up the other. Then the older one comes down to my study: "Let's play!"

That means coats and jeans for everybody, and then into the car. First we stop and pick up donuts for breakfast (and to eat in the car while we drive). Then we pull into a convenience store for a paper. When we finally get back home, the girls munch on donuts and I read the paper for a few minutes before we finish getting ready and head out to church.

Now, I don't know about you, but when I have only a few minutes with the newspaper, I get down to business right away. I read the comics.

Before you lose respect for me as a serious person worth listening to, let me explain. It seems to me that with a few swift strokes of a pen, a cartoonist can capture ideas, trends, and opinions, and convey them intelligently to a large audience. Sometimes this takes eight to ten panels on a page; but occasionally, a single frame goes right to the heart of an issue. Cartoons make a point and have a way of staying with you for some time after you've seen them.

Let me change the image a bit. Think of the last time you listened to someone who was making some sort of speech. It may have been a speaker at a school assembly or a politician on TV. Or maybe it was at church last Sunday. Can you recall what the speaker said? Chances are, if you remember anything, you recall a story or joke that caught your attention.

Making It Memorable

Stories (or illustrations, as preachers call them) make a point in a way that we enjoy. We may like the way it is told, or just appreciate the story itself. Let's face it—we'd much rather hear how a cow kicked over a bucket and then took a swipe at someone when he tried to milk her, than listen to some long, drawn out explanation of the rigors of farm life.

These stories are like cartoons: they make a point in a quick, often funny, way. And the point stays with you.

Jesus knew enough about human nature to appreciate the simple fact that people like stories. The Gospels are full of stories that He told. They punctuate His teaching, like comics in a daily newspaper. And like the comics, Jesus' stories captured the interest of His listeners.

The stories Jesus told are called parables in the

Gospels. The Synoptic Gospels especially are full of them. Mark says that shortly after Jesus began His public ministry, He used parables exclusively to teach the crowds that followed Him: "He did not say anything to them without using a parable. But when He was alone with His own disciples, He explained everything" (Mark 4:34).

Matthew 13 is devoted to seven of Jesus' parables. There are other places in the first Gospel where Jesus tells stories, but we're going to concentrate on this chapter and look together at five of the seven parables in it. If you haven't read it recently, take a few minutes right now to scan this chapter quickly.

A Difference in Dirt

The Parable of the Sower is found in Matthew 13:1-9. Jesus told a story about a farmer going out to plant some seeds. This seed landed in different places:

- Along the path.
- On rocky places.
- Among thorns.
- On good soil.

In each case, something happened with the seed, depending on where it ended up when it left the farmer's hand. Birds, heat, and thorns all tried to destroy what was sown. Only the seed which fell into good soil produced a crop.

What is the point of this story?

Fortunately for us, Jesus Himself gave an explanation of this parable. Usually, Jesus left His audience to figure out the meaning of what He said, but in this case He offered some help.

Jesus told His audience to think about the soil as the human heart; the four soils are four types of hearts. The seed being planted is the Word of God. The sower is the one who shares the Word. What will happen when the sower scatters his seed on this field? Will it grow?

We planted a small garden in our backyard last summer. First we had to clear away some grass, then break up and fertilize the soil, and finally we were ready to put in the seed.

Once this was done, we covered up the rows neatly and sat back to see what would happen. First, the birds came, seemingly grateful that we had gone to all this trouble for their benefit. Then there were the weed armies, which threatened our small crop (eventually defeating some raspberry bushes). And soon after the plants started poking through the dirt, we noticed cute little bunnies nibbling off the green shoots.

Our seed had been sown carefully, but it had a hard time trying to survive.

One of the principles Jesus was teaching with this parable is that people who hear "the message about the kingdom" (13:19) face very real danger. Jesus knew that many would hear the Gospel, and even be affected by it for a time. But then they would go their own ways.

Three kinds of threats faced the hearers in this parable: (1) The evil one snatched away the seed sown along the path; the hearer did not understand it. (2) Persecution or testing causes some to fall away; these people are the rocky places in the soil—they have no roots. (3) Worries of daily life cause the message to be crowded out of the hearts of others; these people are the soil with thorns (13:19-22).

Some would succumb to the pressures of these forces. But the seed that landed on good soil would bear fruit. These people understand the Word and are fruitful. Jesus talked about good soil which produced a huge crop:

> *But what was sown on good soil is the man who hears the word and understands it. He produces a crop, yielding a hundred, sixty or thirty times what was sown.*
>
> Matthew 13:23

For Jesus—as for Paul, John, and other New Testament writers—the Christian life is one which produces fruit. In other words, a person who hears the message about the kingdom (that is, the Gospel message) should show the effects of a changed life by living a life that pleases God.

The person who hears and receives the Gospel must bear the sort of fruit that Paul describes: "The fruit of the Spirit is love, joy, peace, patience, kindness, goodness, faithfulness, gentleness and self-control" (Galatians 5:22-23). Other evidences of bearing fruit might be to win others to Christ, do good works, share material things, or demonstrate a holy life (see Romans 1:13; Colossians 1:10; Romans 6:22; 15:27).

The message of this first parable is that people have different responses to the Gospel. Only a few who hear the message receive it, understand it, and remain committed to it; they are fruitful.

Small Beginnings

I have a pack of "Wonda-Sponges" downstairs in my workshop. If I drop one of these skinny sponges into a pail of water, it immediately swells to become three or four times its original size. The wonders of modern technology!

The mustard seed in another parable is a little like my "Wonda-Sponge"—a tiny thing becoming very big. This parable is very short, and like most of the parables Jesus told, it was designed to make just one point.

When Jesus said, "The kingdom of heaven is like a mustard seed" (Matthew 13:31), He was giving His listeners one more principle about the way God works. He illustrated the principle with a mustard seed—a tiny speck which grows into a plant large enough to hold birds. The point is that the kingdom starts off looking small and insignificant, like the mustard seed. It is not until the message of the Gospel is planted and takes root in a person's life that the dramatic change takes place: the small seed grows into a large plant that is useful.

This principle can be seen in people like Paul and Silas. Ordinary men were changed when they encountered Jesus. Soon, they were accused of affecting the whole world around them (Acts 17:6).

Another short parable makes the same point. Jesus again used a common item—yeast—to teach about God.

If you bake, you know the importance of yeast. Too little, and bread takes on characteristics of linoleum. Too much, and you get a flavor that defies description. When the amount is just right, then the bread can turn out perfect. Of course, it's not just a matter of dumping the stuff into a bowl full of dough and then waiting for the bread to form. Yeast must be worked into the whole batch of dough if it is to do its job of making the dough rise to twice its original size.

Like the mustard seed, yeast seems to be too small to matter much. But Jesus says that when a person allows the message of the Gospel to permeate his or her life, it can bring about some wonderful—and big—changes.

Who would expect much from a "Wonda-Sponge"? Why would a miniscule seed be worth caring about? How can a small portion of some brown stuff affect the quality of baked goods? You wouldn't expect great things from a sponge, a mustard seed, or yeast. But their effect is greater than their size.

And who would have expected a carpenter from Nazareth to have much of an impact on His society—and on the course of history? Who would have expected Jesus to have the words of life?

I Found It!

Let's look at one last set of parables, in Matthew 13:44-46. As He did with the Parables of the Mustard Seed and the Yeast, Jesus again used two parables to illustrate a single point.

First, He compared the kingdom of heaven to hidden treasure. Then he likened the kingdom to a valuable pearl. In both stories, a person who found the wonderful prize sold all that he had in order to buy something of far greater value.

The lesson here is that the message is tremendously valuable. Just as there was no hesitation on the part of the person who found the treasure or the pearl to trade *everything*, so there should be no hesitation to accept the Gospel and become part of the kingdom. It too is of immeasurable worth. In fact, it is so valuable that it costs everything a person has to get it. It can't be earned, but in giving our lives to God we receive the gift of eternal life.

Something to Think About

Why did Jesus use parables? Why didn't He simply speak plainly? I've already suggested one answer for these questions: Jesus used parables to grab the attention of His audience. He drew elements from everyday life in order to teach lofty spiritual truths.

Another reason that Jesus spoke in parables was to encourage His listeners to think. We hardly ever read about a dialogue between Jesus and another person in which Jesus did all the talking. Rather, Jesus asked questions and He told stories in order to make the other person think. In this way, the person became part of what was going on and did not remain an uninterested observer.

Jesus wants people to think. He wants us to use our minds, to search, to question, to argue. And then, He wants us to recognize and accept the truth. That doesn't mean that thinking stops; no, even after we've accepted the truth and become followers of the Leader, we must still keep thinking and learning.

The Apostle Paul is a good model for us when it comes to thinking. Even toward the end of his life,

Paul could say, "I want to know Christ" (Philippians 3:10). The great apostle was not content with what he had already learned. He kept digging and continued questioning.

Drawing from Experience

Matthew 13 begins with a description of a scene where Jesus was teaching a large group of people. The crowd was so big that Jesus had to get into a boat, where He would be higher up and farther away, to be more easily heard.

By this time in His career, Jesus was popular. He had healed many. He had taken on the religious leaders and beat them at their own game. Jesus had called special disciples from nearby towns—perhaps some who were known to people listening that day.

That day signaled a new approach for Jesus in His teaching. Up to that point, He had been talking directly to the people, as He did in the Sermon on the Mount. Then He drew out something new from His bag of teacher's tools: the parable.

Bible scholars agree that Jesus was the first person to use parables to a great extent. We have no record of parables in the Old Testament, and it may surprise us that no one else besides Jesus used them in the New Testament. Jesus pioneered this method of reaching people in a fresh and exciting way.

Habits, customs, or the assorted paraphernalia of daily life became the starting place for each of Jesus' parables. He took what was common for His audience and used it to draw out some deep, spiritual truth. He went from the known to the unknown.

Parables conveyed a single point. The many details that went into a parable were generally there to make the story interesting, not to make it hard to understand.

We've looked at five parables in this chapter. Each of them has something to say about the kingdom of heaven. Put together, these parables form a composite picture of God—what He is like, what He expects, how He works.

The Parable of the Sower shows how the message that is scattered far and wide ends up taking hold in only a few lives.

The mustard seed and yeast demonstrate that something which appears to be small and insignificant becomes great in God's hand; the Gospel changes lives. Finally, the kingdom is like a hidden treasure, which demands that the one who finds it trade everything, including his very life, to have it.

Parables contain principles for those who follow Jesus. They show that God expects fruit, He promises to work in a disciple's life, and He offers a treasure that is worth any sacrifice.

What do these parables told by the Leader say to you?

A CLOSER LOOK
Matthew 16:1–17:23

CHAPTER NINE

One of the hobbies Sue and I enjoy is refinishing antique furniture. Actually, this is more than a hobby, since we've bought a bunch of old stuff cheaply and cleaned it up. My desk chair was salvaged from a garage sale and stripped of its bright yellow paint. Now it sits in my office, a rich, reddish-brown mahogany, testifying to lots of hard work.

Sue's favorite piece is a chair she rescued from her grandmother's basement. It was one of a larger set, all of which had been painted pink and used for stepstools. After hours of scraping, the original oak wood peeked through. Those chairs had been oak all along, but their wood was hidden beneath layers of paint and dirt.

I think of those chairs when I read in Matthew 17 about Jesus' transfiguration. Standing on a mountain with His three closest disciples, Jesus revealed Himself with the layers stripped away.

The Transfiguration is a highlight of Jesus' public ministry, and we'll talk about it more in a moment.

First, we need to dip into Matthew 16 and look over some of the events that led up to that spectacular display on the mountain.

Prove It!

Matthew 16 opens with a confrontation between Jesus and some religious leaders:

> *The Pharisees and Sadducees came to Jesus and tested Him by asking Him to show them a sign from heaven.*
> Matthew 16:1

These people had made trouble for Jesus already (see, for example, 12:1-14). Now they came to Him again, this time with the pretense of a legitimate request. They wanted a sign that would prove His claim to be from heaven.

In a way, this was a reasonable request. The Jews were expecting the one who would come from God to play an important role in their lives. They looked for that one to substantiate his claim of being from God with some sort of unusual sign.

The problem with these religious leaders was that they had ignored the many things Jesus had already done—things that were intended to show others who He was. Do you remember what Jesus said to the messengers who came from John the Baptist? He told them to tell John about the blind who received their sight and the lame who were walking. These miracles were supposed to prove that Jesus was the One who had come from God (see 11:4-6).

John believed Jesus and followed Him. His brief

lapse while in prison is understandable, and he probably did not waver again after he heard the message from Jesus.

The Pharisees and Sadducees were different. They never professed to believe Jesus. Instead, they constantly challenged Him and tried to disrupt His ministry. They wanted to trick Him into making a mistake.

For these people, Jesus had no kind word. He told them they should be able to recognize the clear signs around them. He said something like this: "Look, just as those who are familiar with weather patterns can predict what the next day will be like, so you who are familiar with the Scriptures should be able to see how God is plainly at work" (see 16:2-3).

When Jesus led His followers away from these religious professionals, He warned them to guard against the yeast of the Pharisees and Sadducees. At first, the disciples did not understand what Jesus was telling them, but eventually they grasped the meaning of His words: "Then they understood that He was not telling them to guard against the yeast used in bread, but against the *teaching* of the Pharisees and Sadducees" (16:12, italics added).

Who Is He?

Jesus took His band to Caesarea Philippi, a small city north of Galilee in the high foothills of Mount Hermon. There they spent some time alone, far from the noisy crowds. During this time, Jesus asked His disciples for the results of an opinion poll they had been conducting:

"Who do people say the Son of Man is?"

They replied, "Some say John the Baptist; others say Elijah; and still others, Jeremiah or one of the prophets."
Matthew 16:13-14

Jesus wanted to know what people were thinking about Him. The answers to His question, though, are a bit surprising.

Mark tells us that it was King Herod who, among others, thought that Jesus was John the Baptist raised from the dead (Mark 6:14). Herod's superstitious nature made him believe that Jesus' miraculous power was the result of His life after death.

Another guess popular in that day was that Jesus was Elijah. This fiery Old Testament prophet was a favorite figure in Jewish folklore. They knew the Book of Malachi: "See, I will send you the prophet Elijah before that great and dreadful day of the Lord comes" (Malachi 4:5). Using this verse as a starting point, the Jews had gone on to develop an elaborate scheme for the end times, a scheme in which Elijah was prominent. They thought Elijah would come immediately before God's Messiah, heralding the Day of the Lord. When people saw Jesus performing miracles and speaking the way He did, they assumed He was Elijah, sent as a forerunner of the Messiah.

Jeremiah was another person who figured in these speculations about the end times. His return is not spoken of anywhere in the Bible; it is strictly a function of that Jewish speculative system.

On the whole, the answers that the disciples gave to

Jesus show that the people of His day were having trouble with their expectations. For those who could think only in terms of a military Messiah, Jesus simply did not fit in. At best, He could function as a predecessor (so some thought) of the mighty one who would come eventually to drive out the evil Romans.

Having an idea of popular opinion, Jesus turned to His own followers and asked: "But what about you? Who do you say I am?" (Matthew 16:15)

Peter spoke for the whole group: "You are the Christ, the Son of the living God" (16:16).

This is the answer Jesus had been looking for. Peter and the others recognized what the Pharisees and Sadducees had failed to see: *Jesus Himself was God's Messiah, the One whom God had sent.* Jesus commended Peter for his answer and made clear that even what Peter said had been given to him by God (16:17).

Why Did He Come?

After this triumphant moment, Peter soon gave in to a completely different leading. Jesus began explaining to the disciples that He must die. Peter actually pulled Jesus aside and rebuked Him:

"Never, Lord," he said. "This shall never happen to You!"

Jesus turned and said to Peter, "Out of My sight, Satan! You are a stumbling block to Me; you do not have in mind the things of God, but the things of men."

Matthew 16:22-23

The disciples were capable of doing great things for God, but at times they came crashing down. When Jesus turned to speak to Peter, He addressed a disciple at his lowest point. He did not say that Peter was actually Satan, but He did condemn the attitude which opposed what God wanted.

Any disciple can give in to the danger of doing something that is against what God wants. Peter here was probably only thinking of Jesus' welfare. Why should Jesus talk about dying? Didn't He know that such talk would lower the morale of His followers?

As we read on in the Gospel, we learn that it was precisely Jesus' death which made salvation possible. He could not afford to give in to Peter's request. Jesus had to go on to the cross, and He wanted His disciples to understand that. They simply could not put their own desires above God's plan.

The Cost of Following Him

The next verses give the essence of what it means to be a true disciple:

> *If anyone would come after Me, he must deny himself and take up his cross and follow Me. For whoever wants to save his life will lose it, but whoever loses his life for Me will find it. What good will it be for a man if he gains the whole world, yet forfeits his soul? Or what can a man give in exchange for his soul?*
> Matthew 16:24-26

Jesus told Peter and the others precisely what God expected from them. These verses outline what is at stake for a person who follows the Leader.

The central requirement for being a disciple sounds strange: Jesus says that one must give something away in order to gain something much better. Life comes from dying, and following God means daily denial.

Does this sound attractive to you?

I must confess that I don't always find this principle an easy one to grasp. I need to keep coming back to these words to remind myself that Jesus said them. Then I realize that even though I don't fully understand how all this works, I can still trust the One who gave the directions. I can still follow Him.

I wouldn't be surprised if even the original disciples had trouble with these ideas. Could they really live by dying? Could they actually give something away and still gain by doing that? Did they really have to take up a cross—be ready to die—in order to be disciples?

If we are to believe Jesus, then we must answer each of these questions with a yes. You'll notice that I said, "If we believe Jesus." Belief is the heart of the matter, and the next story Matthew tells helps us believe.

The Truth Revealed

In some ways, everything that had happened in Jesus' earthly ministry led to this point.

> *After six days Jesus took with Him Peter, James and John the brother of James, and led them up a high mountain by themselves. There He was transfigured before them. His face shone like the sun, and His clothes became as white as the light.*
>
> Matthew 17:1-2

On the mountain, Jesus stood before His special three friends in all His glory. This was a sight that made a deep impression on those who saw it, and each of the Synoptic writers records the Transfiguration in vivid detail. Such a display of Jesus' glory would have reminded Matthew's readers of Old Testament passages like Numbers 6:24-26:

*The Lord bless you and keep you;
the Lord make His face shine upon you
    and be gracious to you;
the Lord turn His face toward you
    and give you peace.*

The Transfiguration shows other connections with the Old Testament besides a reference to Jesus' shining face. The most obvious of these involves the conversation that took place between Jesus and two prominent Old Testament figures, Moses and Elijah. They suddenly appeared there on the mountain.

The lives of these three men—Jesus, Moses, and Elijah—have some striking similarities. All three were commissioned by God for particular tasks, all spent time alone in the desert, all performed miracles, and all had disciples who carried on their work after they left the earth. Some scholars suggest that Moses appeared as the representative of Jewish Law and Elijah represented the prophets.

Jesus stood between the two, and was affirmed by God to be superior to both of them:

A bright cloud enveloped them, and a voice from the cloud said, "This is My Son, whom I love; with Him I am well pleased. Listen to Him!"

Matthew 17:5

The word from God showed that Jesus is above Moses and Elijah. It also cut Peter off mid-sentence as he was offering to build three tents there on the mountain!

Peter's remark about tents goes back to yet another Old Testament idea. The Jews were looking forward to the time when God would come and dwell among them again, as He had done long ago in the desert. Moses had passed on God's command to the people to celebrate their release from Egypt and the subsequent nomadic lifestyle with a yearly festival (Leviticus 23:33-43). The Feast of Tabernacles, as it was called, looked back in time, and it also looked forward because it anticipated God's return to His people.

When Peter saw Jesus in His divine glory, he recalled the background of that Feast. He thought that God had come back to dwell with His people then, so Peter wanted to build a shelter to commemorate that.

But God had other ideas. He spoke from a cloud to correct Peter, using a voice that struck terror into the hearts of the disciples.

When the cloud passed, all returned to normal: Moses and Elijah were gone, and Jesus had returned to His appearance most familiar to the disciples.

The four left the mountain and rejoined the rest of the Twelve. Jesus again predicted His death, but this time He received no rebuke from anyone. They had learned a great deal more about Jesus. They would still have times when their faith was weak, but they were through trying to dissuade Him from His intended course. Instead, they were "filled with grief" to hear that their beloved Leader was about to die (Matthew 17:23).

What It Means Today

What does the Transfiguration have to say to us? Several things, I think. First, it shows us the important link between Jesus and the Old Testament. God had a plan in mind, which He began in the Old Testament. He carried it out through Jesus, as we read in the New Testament.

Second, the Transfiguration teaches us that Jesus is God. This may seem obvious, but we need to be careful that we do not minimize Jesus' divinity. The Synoptic Gospels give us a good idea of Jesus' human nature, but they do not as often stress His divine nature. An event like the Transfiguration forces us to see Jesus as God.

Remember that antique oak chair I told you about earlier? We saw it in the basement and could recognize that it was a chair, but it was only after we had stripped off layers of old paint and varnish that we saw the chair for what it really was.

When Jesus came to earth, He took on humanity because of the task that He needed to perform. And He was completely human. But in some mysterious way, He was also completely divine. The Transfiguration reminds us that we need to be aware of both parts of His nature.

There is a third lesson in the Transfiguration: it made an impression on some of Jesus' disciples. When they saw Him shining like the sun, these three men were aware that they stood in the presence of God Himself.

Peter and John both indicated how they felt when they wrote some books that are part of the New Testament. Peter was keenly aware of Christ's divine power, His glory, and His goodness (2 Peter 1). And the language John used to describe his vision of Christ in heaven (Revelation 1) reminds us of the description of the Transfiguration.

This last lesson should make us ask how knowledge of Jesus' divinity affects us. Does it bring order to our lives as Christians? Does it strengthen our faith? Does it keep us from wanting our own way and make us eager instead to let God have His way? Does it prepare us to take up a cross, deny ourselves, and be willing to lose our lives for His sake?

The Transfiguration affected each of Jesus' disciples; it answered some of their nagging questions about their Leader. The Transfiguration showed them that the One who placed such high demands on them, the One who promised them great rewards—that One could be trusted, because He is God.

I LOVE A PARADE!
Matthew 19:16–21:22

CHAPTER TEN

The Fourth of July parade in a town where I once lived is one of the summer's highlights. Local businesses, schools, and organizations join together to create a spectacle that lasts most of the morning. Main Street is lined with people, and the parade stretches out for miles. Unless you stake out a spot early in the day, it's almost impossible to see the parade at all.

Children squeal and parents cheer as floats and bands pass by. Spirits run high, and everyone is in a good mood. Often the spectators become part of the action as strolling clowns draw them in by talking with them or handing out suckers. Sometimes one of the watchers sees friends or relatives in the parade and shouts out to get their attention.

Jesus' entrance into Jerusalem, the Triumphal Entry (21:1-11), had all the makings of a parade. People were already in a festive mood because this was the time of Passover, one of the three big annual holidays in Israel.

As Jesus rode into town on a donkey, the streets

ences to death. This mother came to Jesus with a special request for her sons. She was the mother of Zebedee's sons, the disciples James and John.

Parents naturally look out for the welfare of their children, but this mother went too far. She presumed that her boys deserved a special place of honor with Jesus.

Her problem was one of attitude, a fact which the other disciples quickly noticed. Why, they wondered, should James and John be singled out for special treatment?

Jesus had an answer which corrected the mother's attitude and challenged His disciples. He said that the place of honor was not in itself important (as the mother thought). And further, it was not His to assign (as the other disciples thought). What *was* important for all these people to realize was the need for an attitude of service, not superiority. Jesus told them, "Whoever wishes to be first among you, must be your slave" (20:27, NASB).

I remember once being on a school trip that lasted several days. We were touring some hot places in the country, and the highlight of a sweaty day was lunch under a shady tree.

One day, I helped prepare and watch over the food we took in the bus. When it came time to eat, I dove in immediately. It was entirely fitting, I thought, for me to eat first. After all, I had fixed the food and watched over it all morning. (And besides, there was barely enough to go around.)

In the end, my stomach won, and I had my lunch. Not long after that, I came across these words of Jesus and felt them challenging my attitude. These days when I go on picnics, I try hard to resist the urge to jump in the front of the line. I try (with a little more success than before) to remember that Jesus wants us to serve more than to be served.

Faith to See

One of Jesus' miracles also drives home the point He is trying to make with His comments on dying.

On His way out of Jericho, Jesus was stopped by a couple of persistent beggars. Jesus and His disciples had come to Jericho for a rest before their final journey into Jerusalem. Jesus was pestered by people who refused to give Him any peace. They yelled so loudly that Jesus could not help but notice them. " 'What do you want Me to do for you?' He asked. 'Lord,' they answered, 'we want our sight' " (20:33).

Jesus was moved by the faith of these blind beggars, and He healed them immediately. This sort of healing was nothing new; Jesus had already restored sight to others. But this particular occasion was different—when Jesus healed these men, He was performing an act symbolic of what was about to happen in Jerusalem.

Jesus was on His way to a city where people should have recognized Him as the Messiah. Instead, they were plotting to kill Him. The religious experts of that day were in a very real sense blind; they could not see who Jesus was. When Jesus reached out to simple beggars who acknowledged Him as the Son of David (20:31), He demonstrated the importance of seeing and understanding the true Messiah of God.

All three of these encounters help to explain Jesus'

comments about death. The rich young man points out the need for giving up everything to God. The mother of James and John helps us appreciate the importance of serving. And the blind men represent all those who have clear vision when it comes to seeing Jesus for who He is.

Hosanna—Save Now!
Having met these people and prepared His disciples for what was about to happen, Jesus entered Jerusalem. As He came into the city, the people gathered and shouted:

Hosanna to the Son of David!

Blessed is He who comes in the name of the Lord!

Hosanna in the highest!

Matthew 21:9

These praises come from Psalm 118:25-27, and were given by people who were expecting a triumphant King. They wanted to be saved from the oppression of Rome. "Hosanna" means "save now." Even though Jesus heard their praise, He had a different program in mind when He entered Jerusalem. He made this clear as soon as He arrived at the temple.

Spring Cleaning
Jesus regularly attended meetings at the synagogue when He traveled through Jewish cities. Jerusalem's

temple was the center of worship for that city, so His appearance there was not unusual.

But when Jesus arrived at the temple, He noticed activities that were not at all appropriate. There were merchants buying and selling, and Jesus said they were making the temple a "den of robbers" (Matthew 21:13). So He made a whip of cords (as we read in John 2:15) and drove them from the temple courts.

Is this the action of a meek man?

Some have used this passage to justify anger on some occasions: if Jesus became angry, shouldn't we?

But we need to see that this episode really teaches more about obedience than it does about anger. Jesus cleared the temple because of the abuses going on there. When He did this, He quoted from Isaiah (56:7) and Jeremiah (7:11) concerning what was appropriate for His house to justify His actions. He did not behave like a person enraged; rather, He carried out what was in accord with God's will. As He had done on so many occasions already, Jesus again obeyed God's commands, which were laid out in the Scripture for all to see.

Jesus' actions also teach us about God's standards. He could not permit the sort of disgrace these merchants brought to the temple. Their flagrant violation of the Law showed that the people of Jerusalem had become lax; what they had been taught in their youth was no longer considered important or binding. A holy God could not allow this willful disobedience.

One summer I worked at a camp supervising the junior staff. Before the campers came, we had a week of orientation, spelling out the responsibilities of each staff person. Even though we made clear what was expected of each one, some still tried to get away with whatever they could.

As camp progressed, I had to sit down and talk with those whose performance wasn't measuring up to what was required. Usually, one chat like this was enough to bring about marked improvement. Unfortunately, one person needed so much watching and correcting that we finally asked him to leave camp.

My experience with these staff members was a little like what Jesus faced when He came to the temple. He confronted a group of people who knew better. They had been taught for years that the temple was a sacred place; but that teaching faded from importance, and no one bothered to correct the wrong. Eventually, the temple turned into a sort of bazaar.

Jesus changed all that.

Matthew tells us that He went into the temple and "drove out all who were buying and selling there" (21:12). The verb used in this verse, "drove out," is rare in the New Testament. In fact, Matthew uses it in only one other place—when he recounts a similar situation.

Jesus faced a different group of people, but ones who had a similar problem as those who had violated the temple. Jesus met them at the home of a man whose daughter had died (Matthew 9).

At the insistence of the girl's father, Jesus traveled to that home. When He arrived there, He ran into some professional mourners. Jesus told them to stop weeping: "The girl is not dead but asleep" (9:24). This statement made them ridicule Jesus, and so He put them out of the house.

Just as Jesus put out the mourners, so He put out

the buyers and sellers who had been in the temple. The reason for this action was the same in both cases: neither group was willing to obey God by taking Jesus seriously.

Standard of Holiness

The principle of obedience to God's commands comes out clearly in the episode of Jesus clearing the temple. A second principle—adherence to God's standards—is also there for us to learn.

When Jesus cleansed the temple, He gave His followers a graphic picture of the holiness that is to characterize the life of a disciple.

Thinking back on this incident later, the disciples remembered an Old Testament prophecy in a psalm of David which they applied to Jesus: "Zeal for Your house consumes me" (Psalm 69:9). They realized that Jesus acted as He did because of His holy nature. He could not stand to see the temple violated by those merchants.

The temple was holy; it was set apart and dedicated to the service of God. When Jesus saw people who ignored its sacred purpose, He was driven to act as He did. He could not stand by idly while the name of God was dragged down.

Jesus teaches us to appreciate the value of what God calls holy. The temple was the place where God's name resided; that made it important—holy. People were not free to set their own standards and adopt whatever attitude they liked when it came to the temple.

The same is true for other things which God calls

holy. In our day, God's holy standards receive more subtle attacks than those which Jesus ran up against in Jerusalem. We should regularly review the guidelines that God has given us in His Word to make sure that we are living by them and keeping holy what God wants holy.

What areas of our lives are covered by God's standards? There are many, but let me point out just two: our bodies and our time.

The Bible teaches how both of these are and are not to be used so as to bring God glory. Do we appreciate the fact that God considers both time and the human body holy? Do we stay away from the people and things that threaten the holiness of these areas of our lives?

How much TV do you watch? What sort of concerts do you attend? What do you do to your body that may hurt it?

Jesus recognized God's holy standards. When they were violated in Jerusalem, Jesus had to act. This should teach us to be careful with both the people and things that affect what God calls holy.

Wanting More

One last event in Jesus' life before He died was meant to teach the disciples an important lesson about their Leader. It happened one morning as they were walking over the Mount of Olives on their way into Jerusalem.

Jesus and His companions had been staying in Bethany, a little village two miles east of the capital. Jerusalem was full of people who had come to celebrate Passover, so accommodations were hard to find. Fortunately, Mary, Martha, and Lazarus, good friends of Jesus, lived in Bethany, and they made their place available. From there, Jesus and the Twelve could easily commute back and forth to Jerusalem.

One morning, as they walked toward the city, Jesus was hungry (Matthew 21:18). In the distance, He noticed a fig tree; He walked over to pluck some of its fruit. But the tree was bare. Then, in the hearing of His disciples, Jesus cursed the tree.

What right did Jesus have to yell at this little tree? Had He lost control? Was the pressure of what awaited Him becoming too great?

The next few verses answer these questions. We learn from them that Jesus wasn't merely angry with the tree. Rather, He wanted to make a point.

For Jesus, the fig tree represented the Jewish people. He was going into a city where the people were celebrating the Passover, one of God's mightiest acts in history. Yet these same people would a short time later clamor for His death. When Jesus spoke to the fig tree, He revealed to His disciples the expectations He had for the people.

Various words and actions of Jesus have already stressed how much He expects His followers to be fruitful. In fact, Jesus went so far as to say that if a person does not bear fruit, that person is worthless in God's eyes.

When Jesus saw a fig tree with no figs, He saw in it a metaphor for fruitless people. The plant wasn't doing what it was supposed to do, so Jesus cursed it. His message was clear: God would not wait forever for people to bear fruit. This message sunk in to the disciples the next day when they saw that the tree was dead. How quietly they must have passed by that spot (21:19-20).

Moving Mountains

Jesus used the occasion with the fig tree to teach another important lesson—one about faith.

Jesus' ability to make the fig tree die was a direct result of His faith in God's mighty power. Jesus did not want His followers simply to do amazing things; He wanted them to have faith in God.

Moving mountains (21:21) isn't the main issue at stake here, just as the disciples weren't meant only to focus on a withered fig tree. What Jesus really wanted was for His followers to be faithful. Their faithfulness would be put to the test in the next few hours, and Jesus was trying to prepare them. Would they remember His words and the things He had just done?

Faithfulness is an important aspect of the modern follower's life as well. Faithfulness means trusting God to care for each aspect of our daily lives. Faithfulness leans back and lets God have the anxiety that comes from planning a visit to the dentist, preparing for a debate, witnessing to a friend, or praying for a sick relative. All of these activities require faith—such faith as Jesus encourages His disciples to display.

CHOOSING THE CROSS
Matthew 22:34–27:56

CHAPTER ELEVEN

We used to live about three blocks from a set of railroad tracks. Commuter and freight trains would roar along these tracks several times each day. One of the pastimes around there was to take a penny, put it on the tracks, and then wait for a train to roll over it. The penny was flattened, as you might expect.

There is a sense in which Jesus' death was a little like that flattened penny. The religious leaders of His day came barreling down on Him, and He simply did not get out of the way. But there is also a sense in which Jesus' death is very different from that penny. A coin has no will; it has nothing to say about whether it gets dropped into a gumball machine or placed on a steel track to be crushed by a train. Jesus, on the other hand, chose to die.

The Apostle Paul explained this violent death with a note of wonder in his voice:

Very rarely will anyone die for a righteous man, though for a good man someone might possibly dare to

117 / CHOOSING THE CROSS

die. But God demonstrates His own love for us in this: While we were still sinners, Christ died for us.
                                            Romans 5:7-8

Paul stressed that Jesus' sacrificial death was an expression of God's love. But what was it that led Jesus to the point of going through all this agony?

Again we find the answer to this question by examining a series of events that took place in Jesus' life.

Love God

Shortly after Jesus rode into Jerusalem on a donkey, cleared the temple, and cursed a fig tree, He was approached by various religious figures who wanted Him to answer some of their questions.

These people rarely had a kind word for Jesus. Most often, they tried to trick Him into saying something that would incriminate Him so they could get rid of Him legally.

Apart from Nicodemus (whose story appears in John 3), the only legal expert who came to Jesus with an honest question is the one we read about in Matthew 22:34-40. Something in Jesus' teaching, tone, or manner attracted this lawyer to Him and made him ask: "Teacher, which is the greatest commandment in the Law?" (22:36)

Pharisees like this man spent their whole lives studying the Law. Their job was to understand its intricacies, and then explain them to the common people so they could obey its commands.

These scholars developed a set of instructions which went along with the Law Moses had received from God on Mount Sinai. These instructions were passed down from generation to generation, and eventually they became as important as the Law itself. However, the very comments which were supposed to help people obey the Law actually became a hindrance. By the time the Pharisees were done with things, there were over 600 rules a person had to obey in order to be considered a good Jew.

Even an accomplished Pharisee had a hard time measuring up to this impossible standard. Little wonder, then, that a lawyer would come to Jesus and ask for His opinion on the matter. Jesus had established Himself as a knowledgeable teacher; perhaps He could shed some light on which of those hundreds of commandments was really the most important.

For the most part, Jesus did not carry on real conversations with the chief priests and elders of the people, or their messengers. But when this particular man came to Him, Jesus was willing to answer his question.

Jesus summed up the entire Law with a single sentence: "Love the Lord your God with all your heart and with all your soul and with all your mind" (22:37). This is a quotation from Deuteronomy 6:5, a verse that Jesus' listeners would have known by heart.

But how did Jesus' response help anyone? How could a person possibly love God in that way?

Love Your Neighbor

According to Jesus, the sort of love He has in mind is possible only when a person follows a second command. This one also comes from the Old Testament (Leviticus 19:18): "Love your neighbor as yourself" (Matthew 22:39).

This second command from Jesus offers good news and bad news. Good news, because by quoting this verse from Leviticus, Jesus shows how His first command about loving God can be obeyed. And bad news, because according to Jesus, we must all love our neighbors.

Jesus described a person's neighbor when He told the Parable of the Good Samaritan (Luke 10:25-37). The point of that story is that a neighbor is one who is near us, one who has a need that we can meet. The Samaritan in Jesus' story did not go out one day looking for a man who had been beaten up by thieves so he could demonstrate his extraordinary love. Rather, the Samaritan simply responded to the need that was right in front of him. In so doing, he illustrated obedience to the command to love your neighbor as yourself.

Jesus knew that there were many people who were difficult to love. Often, some of the most difficult are those who are right next door, or even living in the same house. He quoted the Old Testament to make a point: no one can love God, who is invisible, unless he has in him the ability to love those who are plainly visible.

Love improves family relationships and enhances good feelings toward a neighbor. Love helps other people feel more worthwhile. And most important, love for the people who are nearby is love for God.

Think about this the next time a pesty brother barges into your room and runs off with a fistful of pencils from your pencil mug. Or when a little sister insists on help with dressing a doll. Or when Dad insists that the lawn be mowed this evening. You can love these people! You may think they are "just" family, but Jesus says these people are neighbors who need to be loved. And in loving them, you show love for God, which is the greatest commandment of all!

When Jesus responded to this lawyer, He explained what His mission was all about. Jesus demonstrated the extent of His love for God by the way He treated the people around Him. He loved them so much that He was willing to die for them—and us—a fact which left Paul both bewildered and elated.

Screamers and Schemers

Jesus' willingness to die becomes evident in the final chapters of Matthew's Gospel. There we see the intense reactions of people around Jesus in the last few days before His death.

The crowd, which had previously followed at a distance, came into the foreground to cheer Jesus on (chapter 21). But they were a fickle bunch, and a short time later these same people clamored for His execution (chapter 27).

The religious leaders, like the Pharisees, chief priests, and elders of the people, had also been in the background for the most part. Matthew made their presence felt by showing various interchanges with Jesus; but it is not until this point in the Gospel that we see these guys rising up to condemn Jesus in the strongest possible language (chapters 26–27). Because He was anticipating this strong denunciation,

Jesus let go with an incredible blast against these legal experts.

Blasting the Hypocrites

The Pharisees and teachers of the Law had misled innocent people who knew no better. Their whole reason for being was to direct simple folks through the difficult terrain of God's Law, and they had failed to do that. Because they had done so badly, Jesus had only curses for these men who went so far as to oppose Him. Earlier Jesus had blessed His followers (chapter 5). Now He pronounced woes for His opponents.

Jesus' words were pointed and direct. His primary target was the hypocrisy evident in the Pharisees, but actually His words reach further. No one is immune from the problem of hypocrisy.

As our study of Jesus' life has shown, He practiced what He preached. Jesus reached out to hurting people, healed the sick, and listened to the cries of the poor. He truly loved His neighbor.

The Pharisees and their cohorts, on the other hand, only went halfway. They could preach true words when they expounded the Old Testament, but they were not at all interested in applying those words to their own lives.

They could, for example, talk about the importance of serving others and displaying humility. But when it came to their own daily affairs, these guys loved "the place of honor at banquets and the most important seats in the synagogues" (23:6).

Another problem of theirs was with sacrificial rituals that were part of the Law. Originally, Moses had included laws about cleanliness to remind the people of the importance of approaching God with a clean heart. The Pharisees had taken these laws and twisted them so they applied merely to the condition of hands, cups, and saucers.

This sort of error frustrated Jesus. He told them:

Woe to you, teachers of the law and Pharisees, you hypocrites! You clean the outside of the cup and dish, but inside they are full of greed and self-indulgence. Blind Pharisee! First clean the inside of the cup and dish, and then the outside also will be clean.
Matthew 23:25-26

The Pharisees' hypocrisy was so abhorrent to Jesus because it confused the very people they should have helped. That's why He called the Pharisees "blind guides" (23:24). They were unfit to lead the people.

Jesus was careful to reserve His harsh words for those who were in a position to know better. For those who depended on the Pharisees for help, Jesus had compassion. He actually wept for Jerusalem (Luke 19:41). Matthew tells us why. The Jews had turned against the messengers God had sent to them, and they remained unwilling to draw near to God (23:37). The Pharisees, with their shallow religiosity, were largely to blame for this attitude.

The Final Days

Until His enemies arrested Him, Jesus spent the rest of His time with the Twelve. He tried to comfort

123 / CHOOSING THE CROSS

them by explaining future events (chapters 24–25) and simply by taking the time to talk.

One evening, Jesus was relaxing in the home of a friend in Bethany. During supper, a woman came in and poured expensive perfume on His head. The dinner guests were flabbergasted at this act. Some of the disciples were indignant. Not knowing what else to say, they took issue with the woman for her extravagance.

> *"Why this waste?" they asked. "This perfume could have been sold at a high price and the money given to the poor."*
>
> Matthew 26:8

Jesus set them straight. As He had done several times in the past few days, Jesus interpreted this act in light of His imminent death. He said:

> *Why are you bothering this woman? She has done a beautiful thing to Me. The poor you will always have with you, but you will not always have Me. When she poured this perfume on My body, she did it to prepare Me for burial.*
>
> Matthew 26:10-12

In ancient times, undertakers used perfume to hide the smell of a dead body rather than the chemicals used today. The woman's act, according to Jesus, was the first in a series of perfumings that would follow. This symbolic deed was just one of several that revolved around Jesus at this point in His life, pointing toward His death.

The Last Supper

Earlier in Matthew, we read several parables that Jesus told. Parables were stories that taught a particular spiritual truth, and Jesus used them with great effect.

So far, the parables we have encountered were in spoken form. But parables aren't limited to this sort of expression. There is also a class of acted-out parables in the Gospels.

One example of an acted-out parable is Jesus' cursing of a fig tree. Another one is the Last Supper, described in Matthew 26:17-30. This meal took on special meaning as Jesus filled the ritual with spiritual content for His disciples.

Jesus' Last Supper was eaten at a time when the rest of Jerusalem was celebrating the Passover. It is entirely likely that Jesus and the Twelve were remembering that same feast while they ate.

Each Passover involved a dinner shared by all the members of a family. This meal was a lengthy affair, with several courses of food. During each course, certain questions were asked by the youngest member present, and answered by the eldest. These questions were designed to remind the ones eating of the first Passover, which had taken place years ago in Egypt.

Even the food was symbolic. Bread was baked without yeast because the Israelites had no time for that when they left Egypt. A dish of bitter herbs at the supper reminded the diners of the years of bitterness their ancestors had endured. Four cups of wine spoke of the festive nature of the meal, since wine was a drink for the rich and the free.

As a family ate the Passover meal, the father or a leader of the group would explain the symbolism attached to each dish. These interpretations were a standard part of the meal.

When Jesus sat down to eat with His disciples that night, they no doubt waited for Him to take the role of the leader, answering the questions raised and explaining the history of each bit of food. They had heard these things every year when they celebrated Passover; tonight would be no different.

But Jesus changed the script.

A New Covenant

Instead of explaining various parts of the meal in terms of what had happened centuries earlier, Jesus applied the food to Himself. He took the unleavened bread, for instance, and when He had broken it, began to distribute the chunks among His disciples. Instead of talking about their ancestors who did not have enough time to use yeast in the bread, Jesus said, "Take and eat; this is My body" (26:26).

Jesus did a similar thing with the cup. A Jew would normally have been reminded of the time when he would be able to drink wine all the time, a time when he would be rich and free. But Jesus took one of the cups: "Drink from it, all of you. This is My blood of the covenant, which is poured out for many for the forgiveness of sins" (26:28).

These words were totally unexpected.

The precise meaning of what Jesus said that night has been debated by scholars and theologians ever since. And there is still no universal consensus on an interpretation of these verses.

We have some idea of how to understand Jesus'

words by reading what He said afterward. Clearly, Jesus did not want His disciples to think that they were actually eating a part of His physical body, or drinking what had been flowing through His veins. Such ideas were totally repugnant to Jews, and they made no sense with Jesus Himself being there in physical form.

On the other hand, we should not be quick to assert that Jesus was wanting His disciples to think solely in terms of mere symbolism.

As with so much of Scripture, we need to seek a middle ground in interpreting these words of Jesus. Like the first disciples, we too should be deeply moved when we come to celebrate the Lord's Supper.

Jesus commanded that the Supper was to become a part of regular Christian fellowship. The Book of Acts indicates that it was practiced right from the start within the early church (see Acts 2:46). In taking the Supper today, the full force of all that Jesus accomplished with His life, death, and resurrection should come together to move the believer.

But at that first Supper, the disciples were no doubt a little bewildered. What exactly was Jesus doing? They understood later, after they had had time to reflect. But that night, they still did not fully comprehend that He was about to die.

Betrayed

Only one of the disciples had a feel for what the next hours would bring. He was Judas, the one known in all the Gospels as the betrayer. Judas knew what would happen because he had a big part in orchestrat-

127 / CHOOSING THE CROSS

ing the events of that evening.

While it was still night, Judas left the somber company around Jesus. He went into Jerusalem to round up the troops which would arrest Jesus. Judas had already arranged this capture with the religious leaders and their henchmen. He knew enough of Jesus' itinerary to predict accurately where He would spend the next hours, and that information was worth a lot of money.

Abandoned

Once Judas had gone out, Jesus led His group to a favorite spot in the Garden of Gethsemane, on the Mount of Olives. They had been to this place often, and probably walked through it on their frequent treks into Jerusalem. They were going to the garden for the last time, and Jesus needed the support of His followers.

On their way there, Jesus and Peter had a talk. Jesus predicted that this stalwart fisherman would forsake Him, like all the others who would scatter when Jesus was captured. Peter, in his typically confident way, retorted, "Even if I have to die with You, I will never disown You" (26:35).

Jesus knew better. On this dark night, even Peter the Rock would fall away. Jesus would face His bleakest hour totally on His own.

Arrested

Jesus' prediction about being abandoned came true. First, the three who were closest to Him were unable to stay awake and comfort Him while He prayed (26:40-45). Then when the troops came to arrest Him, "all the disciples deserted Him and fled" (26:56).

Jesus stood alone. The adoring crowds were gone; His closest followers had gone into hiding. Jesus was left on His own to face the wrath of a group that He had rebuked and humiliated with His unyielding message of righteousness.

The trial Jesus went through was for show. The results of His time before a series of judges had been prearranged. He faced both religious and civil rulers, and all agreed: Jesus had to die.

Only one man tried to stem the tide that was running against Jesus. Pontius Pilate, the Roman authority in Jerusalem, recognized that Jesus' enemies were out to get Him and that He had done nothing to deserve the death penalty.

Pilate could not stop the inevitable—the pressure exerted on him was too great. He offered the crowd a chance to free Jesus, in accordance with a custom of the day; but the crowd had already been stirred into a frenzy by the religious men. They were insistent: "Crucify Him!" (27:22)

In the end, Pilate bowed to their wishes. He might have stopped the proceedings by virtue of his authority, but he gave in. Forced to choose between the life of an innocent Man and his own job, Pilate took the latter option. Even though he symbolically washed his hands of the matter, Pilate was still responsible for his choice to permit Jesus' death. He threw his lot in with the rest of those who wanted so badly to kill the Son of God.

Killed

The Roman custom of crucifixion was a gruesome means of death. Generally, a prisoner sentenced to die in this way was first beaten. Then he would carry the horizontal piece of the cross to the place of execution. Soldiers would nail or tie his hands and feet to the rough wood, then pick up the cross and drop it into a hole. Death was slow; it took hours. Usually a person died from suffocation because the weight of his hanging body made breathing impossible.

Jesus was forced to die in this way.

Part of the agony involved listening to the taunts of those who stood nearby to gloat: "He saved others, but He can't save Himself! He's the King of Israel! Let Him come down now from the cross and we will believe in Him" (27:42).

Some of the spectators, though, had only Jesus' best interests at heart. A small group of brave women and men stayed with Him to the end. They heard Him call out, "Eloi, Eloi, lama sabach-thani?" This was a phrase in the Aramaic language, which was commonly spoken by people in Jesus' day. Matthew translated this quote from Psalm 22:1 into Greek for his readers: "My God, My God, why have You forsaken Me?" (Matthew 27:46)

Shortly after this cry, Jesus died. Pain tore at the hearts of His followers. Matthew described a series of events that attested to the cataclysmic effect of this death. An earthquake shook the area, and the bodies of holy people who had died came walking out of their tombs. In the city, the curtain of the temple ripped from top to bottom. This curtain had previously separated the holy of holies from the rest of the temple, but Jesus' death opened a way of access to God.

A Roman soldier standing by the cross took note of these unusual things and remarked, "Surely He was the Son of God!" (27:54)

The followers of Jesus who were gathered at the foot of the cross did not doubt that claim. They knew that Jesus had come from God. But now they had to wonder what was next. Would the puzzling remarks Jesus had made about rising from the dead come true? And what would become of them, now that their Leader was dead?

AN EMPTY TOMB
Matthew 27:57–28:20

CHAPTER TWELVE

Joseph of Arimathea carefully laid the dead body on the stone slab. This Man had been his Leader for some time, and now He deserved respect. Joseph had intended to use this tomb for his own family, but nothing was too good for Jesus. He would have another vault cut one day.

Stepping out of the cool darkness into the bright, hot sunshine, Joseph blinked and then motioned to some of his workers. Together they slowly rolled a large stone over the opening in the rock. A last whiff of sweet perfume drifted out. The tomb was sealed.

Joseph turned to go. He was quiet, thinking about the past few days in Jerusalem and Bethany with Jesus and the Twelve. The same thought kept going through his mind: what now? He looked up and noticed Mary and her friend from Magdala coming down the path. None of them spoke, but their eyes told the state of their souls. Joseph headed for home, while the two women took up their post by the tomb. Nearby, the Roman soldiers who had come to seal and guard the grave looked at the women and smirked. Such foolishness, this sitting and waiting for the impossible....

Mary Magdalene, Mary the mother of James, and Salome returned to the grave early Sunday morning (Mark 16:1). Jesus had been gone less than 72 hours, but already it seemed like ages. They were reflecting again on the things He had taught them. All of a sudden, the ground began to tremble. An angel appeared out of nowhere.

The angel came with a startling message: Jesus was alive! The women listened to him, barely able to believe their ears.

> *Do not be afraid, for I know that you are looking for Jesus, who was crucified. He is not here; He has risen, just as He said. Come and see the place where He lay. Then go quickly and tell His disciples: "He has risen from the dead and is going ahead of you into Galilee. There you will see Him." Now I have told you.*
> Matthew 28:5-7

The women looked into the tomb. It was empty. The angel must be telling the truth! Who would have moved the body? And so they ran, eager to share their good news.

The women did not get far. There, standing on the path in front of them, was Jesus.

Now their joy knew no bounds. They fell at His feet, laughing and crying, delighted and awed. Their Lord *was* alive!

He spoke: "Go and tell My brothers to go to Galilee; there they will see Me" (28:10). It took an effort to tear themselves away, but the women left, eager to find the other disciples.

Cover-up

Matthew interrupts the joyful reunion to describe a tense situation. The Roman guards who had seen the angel (28:4) finally recovered and ran to tell their superiors.

These soldiers had been assigned to guard Jesus' tomb. Failure to carry out their task was punishable by death (see, for example, Acts 12:19). But this particular situation was not so easily solved. If the soldiers were killed because the body was missing, then their deaths would draw attention to Jesus' earlier predictions that He would rise from the dead. The priests and elders could have none of that.

So they devised a plan. They bribed the soldiers and told them to say that Jesus' disciples stole the body during the night (28:12-13). Using an elaborate cover-up scheme, these religious leaders demonstrated their blindness to the end. Even in the face of an obvious act of God—an angel had appeared and the body was gone!—they refused to believe.

The Last Challenge

The disciples reacted differently. They obeyed Jesus' command as relayed by the women, and went to Galilee from Jerusalem (28:16). There they met Jesus at a mountain.

What a joyful reunion that must have been!

Jesus began His public ministry by teaching His disciples on a mountain (5:1). That ministry concluded with another, shorter address on a mountain. This one has been called the Great Commission. It lays out one last set of instructions for the men who had gone through three intense years of training with Jesus.

In this Great Commission, Jesus told His disciples three things. They were to go, show, and know.

Go

Jesus explained to His followers that the first order of business was to contact others with the Gospel. As a result of His death and resurrection, Jesus had authority. This meant that He could tell His disciples where to go and how to act.

> *Jesus came to them and said, "All authority in heaven and on earth has been given to Me. Therefore go and make disciples of all nations, baptizing them in the name of the Father and of the Son and of the Holy Spirit, and teaching them to obey everything I have commanded you. And surely I will be with you always, to the very end of the age."*
>
> Matthew 28:18-20

Jesus' commission to His followers was now more extensive in scope than that of their earlier preaching mission (chapter 10). This time they were to go outside the borders of Israel and make an impact on "all nations."

For three years, Jesus had trained these 11 men. They had listened to Him teach, watched Him respond to a variety of situations, and been impressed by His desire to minister to all kinds of people. Finally the time had come to try their wings—to take what Jesus had taught them and put it into practice.

These disciples were now ready to go out and make other disciples. This word "make" conveys the sense of taking time to work with another person to develop character and faith, the hallmarks of discipleship. Jesus was not sending these 11 men on a mission that would end quickly, or even be done once they had died. Rather, He was laying the groundwork for an enterprise that would survive for centuries.

The old proverb says, "Give a man a fish and he will have a meal; teach a man to fish and he will eat for years." Jesus had taught His disciples to fish; He had given them a wealth of experience to draw on, and equipped them to pass on that valuable training to others. Now they were ready to go out, each one reaching and teaching others.

The Book of Acts describes the effects of Jesus' Great Commission by tracing the steps of just a few of the disciples and their converts. The information in Acts is far from exhaustive, but it is enough to give us an idea of the extent of the ministry of these people. At one point, two later disciples were accused of having an influence that has affected the entire known world (Acts 17:6). That shows the power of Jesus' Commission in action!

Show

Jesus sent His followers out to preach the Good News. As they did this, He expected them to be wildly successful in reaching new souls for God. Earlier, Jesus had said: "Open your eyes and look at the fields! They are ripe for harvest" (John 4:35). At the close of His time on earth, Jesus sent His disciples into those fields to reap that harvest.

Peter is a good example of an effective disciple. Though his faith had wavered when the Romans came to take Jesus away, Peter recovered from this brief lapse and went on to become a mighty preacher. On one day alone, his sermons helped to add about 3,000 new converts to the church (Acts 2:41).

In the early days of the church, a person who professed Jesus as Lord was usually baptized immediately. Jesus commanded the practice of baptism in the Great Commission. Then, as now, baptism did two things.

First, baptism enforces for the person being baptized the reality of a spiritual truth. The convert has confessed faith in God's ability to save, and baptism acts as the physical sign of the spiritual reality of salvation. In this way, baptism is a confirmation of faith.

Second, baptism shows others that a person is placing himself in God's family. The act of baptism is unusual in the general course of life, and it gives testimony to an unusual occurrence in a person's life. In this way, baptism is a demonstration.

By confirming and demonstrating God's action in life, baptism shows that something new and different is going on. Baptism serves as the identity card for a group of people whose membership list is open-ended. This is no private club or exclusive fraternity. Christianity is open to all who believe, and membership in its family is simply shown by the ceremony of baptism.

Know

Jesus gave one last word of comfort to His disciples before He sent them out: "I will be with you always, to the very end of the age" (Matthew 28:20). This comment reminded them of a truth Matthew had noticed when he reflected on Jesus' birth.

Turn back for a minute to the first chapter of Matthew. There we read about Joseph and the part he played. One of Joseph's responsibilities was to name the new baby—to call Him Jesus, as the angel had instructed.

Like others in His time, Jesus also had another name by which He was known. Matthew supplied this because of a connection he noticed between Jesus and a prophecy Isaiah had made centuries before. Matthew looked back and found that Isaiah (7:14) had predicted: "The virgin will be with child and will give birth to a son, and they will call Him Immanuel" (Matthew 1:23a). This was highly significant for Matthew, who wanted to point out that Jesus is God. In Isaiah, Matthew found further proof: this new baby carried a name which meant "God with us" (1:23b).

So right at the beginning of the Gospel, Matthew insists that Jesus is God—God with us. In other words, God, through Jesus, was with His people—watching them, caring for them, teaching them.

Now, at the close of the Gospel, Matthew sounds the same note. He remembers that Jesus sent out His disciples with the promise that He would be with them wherever they went, whatever they did.

They could leave with the confidence that their Leader and Lord went with them. This was a fact, something they could hold on to and know.

We have times in our house when one of the girls will wake up screaming because of a nightmare. When that happens, I go into her room and hold her, and let her know that I am with her. I don't try to explain that she has had a nightmare. I don't even try to convince her that there is no hairy monster on her bed. I just let her know that I'm there. That is enough to calm her and send her back to sleep.

Jesus' promise works the same way. His disciples were about to go out to do hard, scary work. He wanted them to know that wherever they went and whatever they did, He was with them. Because of that, there was no longer any reason to be afraid. They could, and would, do great things.

Wrapping It Up

Follow the Leader—is it a child's game, or a lifelong adventure? How do you judge it, now that you've learned some of the rules and met some players? Have you been drawn into the game because the Leader seemed so attractive? If so, then you have joined with thousands of others who have played and are playing for the same reason.

Matthew's intention all along was to focus on the Leader. Time after time, Matthew pointed at Jesus: here's what He said, where He went, who He touched, how He acted.

Through our study of the Book of Matthew, we were there when an angel came to speak with Joseph. We understood with Matthew how Jesus' birth fit into God's grand scheme of events. We watched as

Jesus grew into manhood.

We imagined ourselves standing on the shores of the Jordan River while John baptized Jesus. Then the sky ripped open, a dove fluttered down, and a voice boomed out like thunder. We knew that this was no ordinary day.

We felt the pangs of hunger as Jesus endured nearly six weeks of solitude in the desert, and we stood by hushed as He methodically dismantled Satan's arguments by using Scripture.

Then we met His first followers: rough fishermen, a tax collector, an activist. They were all unlikely characters. But slowly Jesus molded them into first-rate disciples. There were hard times and good times for these men. Occasionally they doubted Jesus' ability, or just plain did not understand what He was trying to say. But at other times, they had brilliant flashes of insight.

Life wasn't easy for Jesus, either. People frequently demanded His attention, so He would have to sneak away in the morning just to have time alone with God. Too often the crowd seemed interested only in what Jesus could give them; they rarely understood the meaning of His actions.

But how they loved to hear Jesus speak! The stories He told were rich and full, not at all stuffy and obtuse like the words of the Pharisees. In fact, Jesus seemed entirely different from the religious experts they had known. He spoke His mind and didn't shrink away from exposing corruption and hypocrisy.

In the end, this frankness killed Him. The religious leaders could no longer afford to have Jesus chipping away at their authority among the people. He was too big a threat to them. So they plotted against Him.

Their plans were shrouded by the excuse that He was a troublemaker, One who threatened the fragile peace Israel had with Rome. They ignored altogether the clear evidence that God was working in and through Jesus. These legal experts remained blind to the end.

Before He died, Jesus spent some time alone with His disciples. He tried to explain what was about to happen so that they would be prepared. But His followers were too caught up in their own petty affairs.

When the time finally came that Jesus was about to be captured, the disciples fled, confused and bewildered.

Just a few of them watched while Jesus hung on that cross. His body bore the marks of the punishment in which the Romans excelled. The only thing that kept His followers there until the end was the great love they had for their Leader. It was love beyond reason; they probably risked arrest just for attending the execution.

Finally, Jesus died. It was the end of an era, some probably thought—and others certainly hoped so. As Jesus was laid in a newly cut tomb, the dreams of many were put to rest with Him. Some women, however, refused to let go. They maintained a faithful vigil near the grave.

They were the first ones to notice when something unusual happened early Sunday morning. In the midst of an earthquake, an angel (again!) appeared with a startling announcement: Jesus was alive!

The women stumbled back to tell the others. But

they didn't get far. Blocking their path was Jesus Himself. It wasn't over! Jesus was back, and ready to meet again with His disciples.

The Eleven (the traitor was dead now) saw Jesus on one of Galilee's mountains. The experience was one of the high points of their lives. It was there that Jesus gave them their final instructions, their marching orders.

The Domino Effect

Have you ever lined up a few dozen dominoes in a design and then tipped over the first one? What happened? Each one hit the next, and so on, until every one of the dominoes was down.

You might think of Jesus as the hand which tipped the first domino (His early disciples). Then they touched someone else, and so on and so on, down through the years.

The lessons of discipleship which Jesus gave to the Twelve were supposed to be passed on. Jesus made this clear with His Great Commission. These principles were then picked up by subsequent followers for centuries until they came into our own day.

Now it's time to ask: Are you going to be one of the dominoes? Are you going to be touched by Jesus' instructions on discipleship? Will you in turn knock down another domino?

In Matthew's Gospel, you have met a Leader like no other. He is perfectly trustworthy, completely reliable, loving, interested, and kind. And He holds out a hand to you, inviting you to follow Him.

MORE GREAT BOOKS FROM SONPOWER

Life-in-Focus
Filling Up Your Think Tank by Bill Stearns. What's on your mind? This book will help you explore your thoughts and start thinking the way God wants you to. Find out how important your mind really is. Textbook **6-2264**

Home Sweet Battleground? by Pamela Heim. This book will help you learn how to communicate honestly with your parents. You'll understand them better and find out how to help them see things your way too. Textbook **6-2586**

Caution: Christians Under Construction by Bill Hybels. Build your relationship with God with the tools in this book. It will help you work on your self-image, friendships, perseverance, and more. Textbook **6-2759**

Word-in-Focus
Faith Workout by Bill Myers. Exercise your faith and watch it grow stronger with this study of the Book of James. Stretch your faith in such areas as temptation, the tongue, and money. Textbook **6-2265**

New and Improved by James Long. You can have a better life—a better you—with God's help. This study of 1 John explores your tough questions about truth, love, doubt—living a better life God's way. Textbook **6-2590**

Leader's Guides with Multiuse Transparency Masters and Rip-Offs are available.

SonPower®
Youth Sources

Buy these titles at your local Christian bookstore or order from SP Publications, Inc., Wheaton, Illinois 60187.